You're excited about your future. You have a vision for your life, each step precisely calculated to reach your destination. You're ready to proceed, steady on course, when, out of nowhere, something stops you in your tracks. You're confused, concerned, and unable to make sense of this place you're in. Now what? Dr. Mark Chironna is one of the most intellectually brilliant men I know, and, in his newest book *LifeQuest*, he blazes a path of discovery into, as he so profoundly puts it, "the nowhere between two somewheres." I strongly recommend this book to help you navigate through life's journey!

—*Dr. Ché Ahn*
Apostle, Harvest Apostolic Center, Pasadena, California
Senior Pastor, HRock Church
President, Harvest International Ministry
International Chancellor, Wagner Leadership Institute

As I read Dr. Mark Chironna's *LifeQuest*, it all became clear to me. Had I understood how to navigate "the gap" earlier in my life, I would've been much further down that road by now. Dr. Chironna provides you with a "GPS" for navigating through the gap to your destiny. Read it, and get copies for all those you love.

—*Dr. Samuel R. Chand*
Author, *Leadership Pain*
www.samchand.com

The definitive road map to personal transformation. Mark Chironna's profound insights are anchored by the transcendent realities of the human soul. In *LifeQuest*, he brilliantly provides guidance toward a new future, and, more important, the spiritual key to the strength needed for following his crucial directions. This powerful book is indispensable to all who seek their true destiny.

—*Rabbi Daniel Lapin*
American Alliance of Jews and Christians

D0963424

As a student of life, I am curious to learn from a wise navigator who has mastered the oceans of change. In *LifeQuest*, Dr. Chironna provides a compass that will point anyone toward their destiny. He coaches us through the gap by empowering us to make significant course corrections as we unearth our greatness. This is more than a book. It's original thinking in a sea of annoying echoes. I love it and will recommend it to everyone I know.

—*Simon T. Bailey*
Executive advisor, career mentor, and keynote speaker
Author, *Shift Your Brilliance*

Dr. Mark Chironna is a master at helping people to navigate the shifting waters we call "life." In *LifeQuest*, he will help you to examine the questions you are asking yourself and to reach out to the unknown—to reach the destination for which you were created. As you read this book, get ready to discover the life you were created to live.

—*Benny Perez*
Lead pastor, The Church LV
Las Vegas, Nevada
www.thechurchlv.com

Dr. Chironna has produced another thought-provoking, inspirational handbook for those eager to experience the life they were born to live. *LifeQuest* will take you on the important journey of uncovering your capacity, releasing your creativity, and courageously moving toward your best future. Engaging this resource will change your life!

—*Dominic J. Russo*
Founder, Missions.Me and the "1Nation1Day" vision
www.dominicrusso.com

As with every book he's written, Dr. Chironna has the uncanny ability to uncover keys to escaping a life full of limitations and to flee "liminality," ready to embrace your next rite of passage. If you want to traverse the gap between your current state of reality and your ultimate destiny, don't miss his newest book *LifeQuest*. "When the student is ready, the teacher appears," and Mark Chironna's book has appeared at the perfect time.

—*Delora and Dennis OBrien*
Los Angeles, California

LifeQuest is a beautifully written book with useful stories and practical strategies for navigating the course of your life, even when you are blown off course. Mark uses the metaphor of sailing on a life journey elegantly and with deep meaning at an intellectual, emotional, and spiritual level of understanding.

—*Dr. Patrick Williams*
Director of Training, www.lifecoachtraining.com
Founder, www.coachingtheglobalvillage.org

We all exist in a gap between the "here and now" and the "still to come." In *LifeQuest*, Dr. Mark Chironna expertly guides the reader on a journey of self-awareness and discovery toward fulfillment in life by masterfully using proven human development and coaching techniques. He invites and challenges each reader to overcome fears and to embrace personal empowerment and achievement. I highly recommend this valuable resource to those who are ready to make better decisions and attain better outcomes in any area of life in order to face the future with confidence, expectation, and joy!

—*Dr. James S. Vuocolo*
Master Certified Coach

Mark Chironna's new book, *LifeQuest*, will awaken you to the depths of your life calling and will inspire you to embrace your God-given purpose. *LifeQuest* offers a beacon of hope to those floundering in a sea of indecision and hopelessness, and it will shift the very foundation of what it means to come into agreement with the Kingdom of Heaven to fulfill your destiny. If you want to be challenged and equipped to change the way you live, then this book is for you!

—*Kris Vallotton*
Co-Founder, Bethel School of Supernatural Ministry
Author, *The Supernatural Ways of Royalty* and *Spirit Wars*
Leader, Bethel Church, Redding, California

LifeQuest

MARK CHIRONNA

LifeQuest

WHITAKER
HOUSE

All Scripture quotations are taken from the King James Version of the Holy Bible.

LifeQuest:
Navigating the Gap Between Your Current Reality and Your Future Destiny

www.markchironna.com
https://www.facebook.com/drmarkchironna
https://twitter.com/markchironna

ISBN: 978-1-62911-283-1
eBook ISBN: 978-1-62911-284-8
Printed in the United States of America
© 2015 by Mark J. Chironna

Whitaker House
1030 Hunt Valley Circle
New Kensington, PA 15068
www.whitakerhouse.com

Library of Congress Cataloging-in-Publication Data (Pending)

No part of this book may be reproduced or transmitted in any form or by any means, electronic or mechanical—including photocopying, recording, or by any information storage and retrieval system—without permission in writing from the publisher. Please direct your inquiries to permissionseditor@whitakerhouse.com.

1 2 3 4 5 6 7 8 9 10 11 **W** 22 21 20 19 18 17 16 15

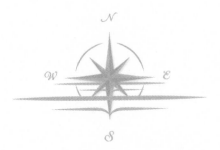

Contents

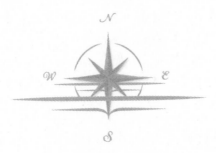

Foreword

One of the strangest memorials ever dedicated to those who served their country in war stands outside the entrance to my former junior high school in Gloversville, New York. "The Thinking Doughboy Statue" was dedicated in 1923 to commemorate the soldiers of World War I. In large letters, the top of the inscription reads Lest We Forget. The uniqueness of the statue is in what we are to remember.

"The Thinking Doughboy" was the creation of artist Karl Illava (1896–1954), who himself knew the hell of war from his service in World War I as a sergeant in the 107th infantry. But unlike Illava's other war memorials, the most famous of which is on the periphery of Central Park in New York City, this one does not depict the bravery, sacrifice, or camaraderie of those who fought the "war to end all wars." A bronze figure of a doughboy is seated on a square ledge atop a square granite base. The right hand of the doughboy is propping up his torso from behind, while his left hand holds a German helmet in front of him. His gaze is directed downward, pensively, much like Rodin's more famous "The Thinker," except that "The Thinking Doughboy" is not nude but in full World War I uniform, with his knapsack, canteen, helmet, and bayonet hanging on his back, and his gas mask draped around his neck.

One question seems to scream forth from all the bronze and granite: "Why?" Here is a war memorial that does not celebrate the victories or the sacrifices of battle, but one that enters that murky zone of questioning the glory and honor bestowed upon its participants and of entertaining doubts about the very enterprise of war itself.

Mark Chironna is an artist of words, not of bronze and granite. But he has produced another "Thinking Doughboy" monument by writing this book. In academic circles, what he describes is called "liminality," a concept that Ludwig Wittgenstein argued comes with a twin: "marginality." One of the many gifts of this book is that Chironna explains liminality in terms that all of us can understand. When soaking in a bubble bath of beliefs suddenly turns into a fire walk of doubt, ambiguity, uncertainty, questioning—-that's the liminality.

If you want to understand God in human terms, or to bring Him down to earth, you don't need liminality. But if you want to understand God on His own terms, if you want to pierce the clouds and allow God to raise you up to divine levels, then you need liminality. Liminality is the wetlands of faith. It is a murky time and a messy place of swampy boundaries, of overlapping ecosystems, of bursting lines, but also a place of honest searching, where illusions cease and truth comes clean. No wonder the Greek god of the ancient world, Hermes—the intermediary between humans and the Olympian gods—presided over transitional times and liminal spaces.

There is no creativity without liminality, for it is the very play of opposites and overlapping lines that gives us the imaginative space in which we can conceive radical alternatives to the status quo. Of course, the greatest imaginative space conceivable is *the future*, and this is where Christianity shines the brightest. Within the heart of Christianity beats liminality, for the circulatory system of the body of Christ is a wetlands of faith and doubt, change and continuity, past, present, and future.

The atheist celebrity-scientist Richard Dawkins has insisted, "I am against religion because it teaches us to be satisfied with not understanding the world." When it comes to Christianity, nothing could be further from the truth. One of the liminalities of the Christian religion is the paradoxical affirmation that the future has already been accomplished. The Catholic

Church, in both its Western and Eastern forms, makes this boundary-crossing explicit in the Eucharistic prayers at every Lord's Supper, in which followers are told to "remember their future." *Anamnesis* is one of the most complex and corrupted Greek words ever to be translated. "To remember" means more than not to forget, or not to forget the future, or to remember to brush your teeth. To "remember our future" is to bring the future into the present more than the past. Our story is one of a future already accomplished in the past, which we celebrate in the present. And we wonder why people don't "get it"? Most Christians don't "get it," either. For Christians, the arrow of time does not go in a one-way direction.

For followers of Jesus, a trip down memory lane is a journey into the future that has already been accomplished. *"And, lo [remember], I am with you always, even unto the end of the world"* (Matthew 28:20).

Chironna's challenge in this marvelous book is for us not to be afraid of lifting anchor and setting sail on the liminal seas, for it is in that churning, heaving, unpredictable space of creative formation that metamorphosis takes place. Sure, there will be times when we will be submerged, even shipwrecked. But Jesus turns shipwrecks into spaceships.

—*Leonard Sweet*
E. Stanley Jones Professor, Drew University
Distinguished Visiting Professor, George Fox University
Distinguished Visiting Professor, Tabor College
Author, *The Well-Played Life* and *Jesus Manifesto*

Introduction

Are you perched on the living edge of the unknown? Do you feel stranded on strange seas without a map or a compass, drifting rudderless through waters where nothing works the way it used to or feels the way it used to or looks as good as it once did?

"Yes," you say, "and I want out."

I know. Everyone does. *The gap*—the tense, trackless ocean that every life crosses—is no day at the beach. Yet there it is, and there you are. You can back away and blow it off. You can spend an entire lifetime avoiding it. But your relief will be temporary, and your search for fulfillment will never end.

The bare, naked truth is that unless you are content to burrow back into familiar places and become their prisoner, you must navigate the gap. Oh, it might get messy; at times, you will feel out of control. That is the nature of the gap, a necessary part of the package. Accept it, and you'll enter the portal to where you really want to be. But the only way to reach your destination is to navigate.

As a baby boomer with some hits and misses under my belt, and as a life coach who helps others sail their strange seas, I get to witness the process more often than most people do. No two situations are identical, but they all share common features. Often, the gap opens when you least expect or want it to. Just when you think your ducks are in a row and you have aligned the direction of your life perfectly, here comes the gap, out of nowhere. Instead of gliding on glassy waters, you find yourself tacking up through an invisible wind, zigzagging the sea without the slightest clue as to why.

If that is where you are, I get it. At some point, every human being can relate to your predicament. Some have backed away, perplexed and unwilling to fare any farther. Others have caught glimpses of something ahead, a tiny spark of a life worth pursuing. So, they slathered on the sunscreen and zigzagged onward.

My guess is that you tried to circumvent your gap, at least at first. Who wouldn't? Yet you picked up this book. You are not quite ready to settle for where you have already been. You might feel like a mess…your world might be on its ear, but your sunscreen is on, and the unknown is nudging you forward. You want to back away, but the gap is sending out a signal. It is faint, yet it hints of promise. It says that the gap you fear just might be an opportunity in disguise. It says that you did not come this far to forfeit the potential you suspect is wrapped in your future. It says that if you turn back now, you will never know what might have been.

Yes, there is a navigator in you, and the gap is yours to take.

What is tacking?

Merriam-Webster's 11ᵗʰ Collegiate Dictionary describes *tacking* in the nautical sense but also explains it in everyday terms. It says that to tack is "to modify one's policy or attitude abruptly."[1] Navigating the gap means making unexpected changes and finding unexpected pathways to your desired destination. Embrace the risk, and you will "taste" the prize.

The Search for Meaning

Navigating does not happen in a vacuum. The mysteries of the human journey are about *meaning*. Whether we realize it or not, we are engrossed in the search for meaning. We wrestle with all kinds of questions, and we never run out of new ones to ask. Like children who want to know why the sky is blue and how the day turns into night, we keep asking: *Why was I born? How did that happen? Who's in control? Why do good people suffer? What do my children's tendencies reveal about them? How did I end up here? Is this all there is? Why not me?*

The drive to make meaning is inherently human. We cannot help but do it. In fact, we were created to do it. Even when it is unconscious, the search for meaning is high on our list. We want our lives to count, so we strive to know what life means. Our dreams and values matter to us, and we want to know why and how they fit into the bigger picture. When obstacles challenge our progress, we inspect them. We want to know what they reveal. Are they there to help us change course, or should we blow them to pieces and forge ahead?

The belief that our lives are meaningful keeps us keeping on. It is the reason we pursue career paths and start families. Because we believe that life has meaning, we instinctively act to preserve it. When a neighbor's house catches fire, we run to render aid. When a friend or a loved one dies unexpectedly, we search our hearts to know why, how, and how things might have ended differently. Even highway gawkers have a deeper reason to look. They scan the wreckage in search of meaning. They strain their necks not just to see what happened but also to understand it. They run through the what-ifs: What if somebody was hurt? What if somebody died? What if that were to happen to me?

The awareness of meaning triggers our choices. We give money to charities because the needy matter. We muster the courage to make tough decisions because the outcomes are meaningful. We strive to improve our lot because we believe our efforts count for something. Aspiring doctors exchange sleep and immediate financial gain for the rigors of medical school, knowing their sacrifice will eventually help others. Patients make difficult choices, too. When unwelcome diagnoses force them to decide how to proceed, many undergo radical and even painful treatment plans. They do it for one reason: Life means something.

To find meaning is to find the connection between ourselves and everyone else. We need to know where we belong and how our efforts affect our world.

Whether or not we are people of faith, we are curious about eternal things. Even if we try to shelve our spiritual questions, our subconscious minds continue to wonder.

Meaning touches everything we touch. Our desire to be productive springs from our search for meaning. We go to work believing (or, at the very least, *hoping*) that what we do matters. We want to know that our pursuits are leading somewhere, so we embrace opportunities to thrive. The prospect of a raise or a promotion inspires us and tells us that we are making progress, and that progress is meaningful.

Milestones *mean* something. Birthdays remind us that we are on a journey so significant that it continues even beyond our last breath. Anniversaries declare that our relationships affect all that we do. Retirement helps us to understand where we have been, what we have accomplished, and which endeavors are still ahead.

Significant life events such as these update our search for meaning. The meaning of happiness at age five is different from the meaning of happiness at age fifty-five. The word *love* means something different to a newlywed couple from its meaning to a husband and wife celebrating their golden anniversary. The search for meaning has no end date. As long as we possess the cognitive power to pursue it, the search continues.

Meaning in the Gap

It is no wonder that we reel upon finding ourselves at the gap. When meaning is turned on its head, alarms sound deep within us. Like a toddler who sears his tender finger on a hot stove, we shrink back. The gap is too painful for our taste, too inside-out for our sense of order. So, instead of updating the meaning catalog with the new information the gap offers, we resist the gap and everything attached to it.

Yet we cannot resist forever without searing our hearts. You and I were not born for stagnation, and we know it. The gap challenges our idea of what a standstill looks like. It defies our notions of progress and success. The gap feels like stagnation, so we recoil from it. Our souls scream, "Something is *very* wrong here! Surely, progress doesn't look like this."

Convinced that we have taken a terrible detour, we retrace our steps, looking for familiar territory and for old paths toward progress. But the shelf life of the old ways has expired. The levers that worked so well in the past cannot be connected to the new grid. At best, yesterday's tricks will produce mere facsimiles of progress.

The real thing is found only in navigating the gap.

The meaning of the gap becomes clear when its navigators come to terms with uncertainty. Instead of dismissing the unfamiliar, they learn to approach the new paradigms that clash violently with their existing mindset. They suspend their disbelief long enough to step out of themselves and into strange new places of promise.

The gap you have entered probably looks like nothing you would have consciously designed. And how could it? The gap is an innovative state you could not have seen or understood from your previous vantage point. That is why it rubs you the wrong way. You think the gap is working against you. You fear that it will ruin you, your reputation, or your plans. But if you will trust the experience long enough to become a gap navigator, you will learn that both the gap and your destiny are counterintuitive for a reason.

The Twenty-First-Century Paradigm

Today, more than ever, change is the norm. The twenty-first-century reality shifts so rapidly, we can barely make sense of it. News cycles are frenetic. Elections defy expectations. Terrorism has rewired politics and power structures so that even Egypt, a nation with ancient roots, has been brought to its knees. Globalization forces regional problems to cascade across international lines, so that the financial instability of small nations can threaten countries many times their size. Technological advances are made almost daily, so that the phone you bought today is superseded tomorrow, and the way you communicate is changing all the time. Radical innovations like 3-D printing and digital currencies so upend our ideas of how life should work that we question what is possible and even what is real.

This climate of change creates more choices. As a twenty-first-century earth-dweller, you have more choices than your predecessors could have imagined. You probably like it that way. The more alternatives you have, the more you can customize the "command station" that is your world.

But having options presents challenges, too. The more options you have, the less predictable life becomes. In the days of the popular show *Father Knows Best*, for example, the nuclear family was the norm. Home after home was occupied by a married mom and dad with an average of 2.2 children. Jim Anderson, the father who knew best, would hardly recognize today's choices. Will you choose a "traditional" lifestyle or a "nontradition-al" one? Will you enter into a heterosexual marriage, or will you marry a member of your same sex? Will you marry at all, or would you rather just cohabitate? If you have children, will they grow up in a two-parent household, or will you parent them alone? Will you have sole custody, or will your children's time be split between Mom and Dad, Dad and Dad, or Mom and Mom?

Can you see how the range of choices and the pace of change also make meaning a moving target? No sooner do you think you understand something (whether it is marriage, parenthood, the family unit, or any other issue) than the reality changes, and meaning is rendered uncertain again.

Let's follow the thread a little further. The less predictable your life becomes, the more uncertainty you experience. You already know how uncomfortable *that* is. Uncertainty can leave you feeling less in control, and losing control is not most people's idea of comfort!

Ah, but discomfort is the only furniture you will find in the gap. The safe and the familiar don't fit there. The gap demands a counterintuitive approach. That is why most people reject the place. They prefer the soft settee of the comfort zone. The preference is understandable, but so is its outcome. *You cannot cling to the safe and familiar and expect your life to change.*

In the end, you can settle for what is, but you don't have to. In the coming pages, you will discover insights to breakthrough to help you release your grip on the familiar so that you can embrace the gap. You *can* dance your God-given dance all the way to destiny, even in the twenty-first century.

Take a mental snapshot of today's world. What aspects of modernity challenge your grasp of meaning? What makes these points stand out?

Change Is Not Your Enemy

The gap you are in is not the first one you ever encountered. Some gaps are navigated unconsciously. Some are fleeting. Others take more time.

Memorable life experiences help us to understand the feelings that arise when change invades our space. Do you remember the transition you made out of your childhood home environment and into the university setting? Even if you welcomed a new routine, you probably found the change intimidating. You lacked any frame of reference for it, and you had no way of knowing how things would turn out. You wondered whether you could handle being out "on your own."

The adult response to change is not much different. Even if singing at La Scala was your lifelong dream, your first appearance on that hallowed stage would be unsettling. The greats would flash before your mind, and their voices would echo there without mercy. Butterflies would flutter in your midsection. Your palms would sweat. Your knuckles would turn white. Even the voice that had brought you there might rebel at the pressure.

But would you opt out of such an experience, just to avoid the uneasiness of it? I hope not! The fact is that change is not your enemy. Imagine if you had never ventured beyond familiar places. How would your life look today? How many opportunities would you have forfeited for the sake of safety and comfort? What blessings do you enjoy today that would have been missed? Marriage? Children? Career? The freedom to explore life? The satisfaction of overcoming adversity?

Not All Change Is Good

Don't misunderstand me; change *is* vital, but not all change is for the better. Do you remember the inalienable rights listed in the United States' Declaration of Independence? They are life, liberty, and the pursuit of happiness. Most of us can rattle them off because they are ingrained in our national ethos.

Our nation's founding fathers made the importance of these rights plain when they named their author: the Creator. The Declaration's careful listing demonstrates our rights in perfect order. The pursuit of happiness does not come first, although many people give it first place in their lives. Even liberty does not command the first rung of the ladder. The first and foremost right is the right to life itself.

Unless life has meaning and is cherished, the rest of the ladder gives way, and all hope of liberty is lost—not just theoretically but practically, too. After all, if taking someone's life is seen as "normal," what incentive is there to protect the "lesser" freedoms of liberty and happiness? And how can we pursue happiness in an environment stripped of liberty? The truth is that we would not be *free* to do so. The pursuit of happiness would become theoretical—more a poetic term than a protected promise.

This downward spiral is relevant, because we are becoming increasingly dismissive of the right to live. This is not a political statement; it is merely the observation of a sign that we are losing our moorings and our grasp on meaning itself.

The Existential Vacuum

We are born as meaning-makers. Where meaning is unclear or missing altogether, we try to clear it up or to fill the void, as the case may be. Deep down, we *know* there is meaning in our experiences and our world, so we search for it. When our search bears no recognizable fruit, we experience *crises of meaning*.

Austrian neurologist and psychiatrist Viktor Frankl explained how the sense of meaninglessness can permeate a person's entire life. His perspective was rooted in twentieth-century realities, but his insights are applicable even today:

> Because of social pressure, individualism is rejected by most people in favor of conformity. Thus the individual relies mainly upon the actions of others and neglects the meaning of his own personal life. Hence he sees his own life as meaningless and falls into the "exis-

tential vacuum" feeling inner void. Progressive automation causes increasing alcoholism, juvenile delinquency, and suicide.[2]

Frankl saw the *existential vacuum* as a byproduct of industrialization. Yet every epoch is a petri dish in which the culture of meaninglessness can grow. Our times create similar disconnections, and even greater ones. Technological advances, while they have improved the speed of our communications, have caused our interactions to become more impersonal. With authentic relationship on the decline, the ability to watch the world from home becomes an accepted substitute. Meanwhile, we become decreasingly relational and increasingly self-absorbed.

Modern materialism also produces crises of meaning. Unless their core values are rock solid, high achievers who accumulate accolades and wealth are still left wondering what their *real* purpose is. Many who seem to "have it all" yearn for the basics: loving relationships, contentment, peace, and spiritual connectedness. The existential vacuum leaves both the well-heeled and the wishful in want.

At our very core, we value the spiritual over the material. For example, we innately prefer to be driven by values than by money. Values (including matters of faith) hold deeper meaning for us than do material possessions. Money comes and goes, and its buying power rises and falls, but values steady us. Life is not seen as random but as meaningful. With this conviction established, the existential vacuum must close, while vision, mission, and purpose are free to thrive.

Nihilism in the Vacuum

In the existential vacuum, our natural instincts and social traditions fail us. When we search for their guidance, we come up empty and become unsure of what we *ought* to do. Without an end result in mind, it is difficult or even impossible to be decisive. Initiative dwindles, and even the sense of what we *want* to do evaporates. Convinced that nothing matters, we end up following others who are equally lost. We conform ourselves to whatever norms we can find, even when they lead to more of the emptiness that already consumes us.

As a survivor of the Holocaust, Viktor Frankl knew how far the existential vacuum could reach. He had witnessed firsthand how a world without meaning can lead everyday people to reject religious and moral principles. He had watched as the erosion of principles led to the acceptance and justification of heinous acts. In the slaughter of the Jews and other "enemies" identified by Adolf Hitler, Frankl and the rest of the world witnessed one of history's most brutal rejections of the right to life, as tyranny threatened not only Europe but the entire globe.

The entrenchment of the existential vacuum is insidious. It naturally desensitizes us to dark realities and provides convenient cover for our denial, so that many are sucked in unawares. The social climate that fosters such outcomes is a belief system known as *nihilism*. In part, it is defined as "a viewpoint that traditional values and beliefs are unfounded and that existence is senseless and useless...a doctrine that denies any objective ground of truth and especially of moral truths...."[3]

Nihilists embrace the icy belief that life (and all that life entails) is meaningless. Many who flaunt nihilistic lingo are not true nihilists. Yet events in our day prove that the condition has permeated the twenty-first-century culture. The world is rife with nihilistic thinking, so that the killing of millions in the womb is easily justified, and the existence of objective truth is systematically denied.

Wondering Is Not Wandering

So, what does all this have to do with the gap? It is all tied to the importance of meaning. Finding yourself in the gap does *not* make you a nihilist, even though it is in the gap that the search for meaning intensifies. The more aware you are of your need to make meaning, the better equipped you will be to make the gap work *for* you instead of *against* you.

This is your journey, and you get only one. If you wonder why you have more questions than answers, start navigating! Capitalize on the questions that keep you up at night. Follow your curiosity into the gap and beyond—even if you have to tack upwind to do it.

Remember, change is not your enemy. And neither is uncertainty. Allow life's unsettled waters to force open the channels you have kept comfortably closed in your heart and mind. Allow yourself to wonder. Realize that your wondering does not mean you are wandering. Your questions are not silly. They are not time-wasters or sideshows distracting you from what you are "supposed to be doing." They are clues to where you are going. They will reveal what belongs on your path, and what does not.

Your gap—the "nowhere" between two "somewhere"—goes against your grain; but don't let that dissuade you from seeking out its treasure. Examine your questions. Explore the gap. The real distractions, even the ones you do not yet suspect, will soon slough off.

In the end, you will thank your gap for getting in your face.

Notes

1. *Merriam-Webster's 11ᵗʰ Collegiate Dictionary*, electronic version, © 2003, s.v. "tack."
2. Viktor Frankl, *Man's Search for Meaning*, https://www.goodreads.com/quotes/tag/meaning-in-life.
3. *Merriam-Webster's 11ᵗʰ Collegiate Dictionary*, electronic version, © 2003, s.v. "nihilism."

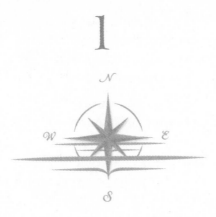

Hello to the Rest of Your Life

Musical greats Sarah Vaughan, Frank Sinatra, and others asked the rhetorical question, "What Are You Doing the Rest of Your Life?"[1] This compelling query spikes the heart rate of people in love, but it inspires another kind of adrenaline rush for those who feel adrift on the seas of life.

The question need not overturn your raft. It is a navigating question, and the answer is closer than you think. But first, let's deal with your expectations about your journey. What does the gap signal to you? Is *feeling adrift* the same as *being adrift*? Is your creeping uncertainty a sure sign you're about to go under?

Before you answer, consider the following question, commonly attributed to Joseph Campbell: "If the path before you is clear, you're probably on someone else's."[2] Don't let the hint of sarcasm throw you off. His statement is both ironic and encouraging. It says, "Don't panic when your path is not clear. It's not supposed to be!"

Whether Campbell's words speak to you about the presence of obstacles or the lack of a clear mental picture (or both), the truth in his statement is powerful. Somehow, we grow up expecting the path to our destiny to be pristine and free of doubt. We assume that the "right path" will never raise any questions. We know clarity is important, and success involves a measure of clarity. But the expectation of uninterrupted clarity is erroneous. If you demand it, you will see yourself as a failure, when you should actually validate many of the quirky places along the way.

Those quirky places are not random. Even your gaps pop up for a reason. They grab your attention because you need to notice them. They look and feel like void places, but they are not empty. They are places of provision, and portals to the rest of your life. When you approach them with intentionality, they strip you of extra baggage and endow you with fresh perspectives for the journey. When you cross the gap, you leave behind groupthink and discover original thought. You quit striving for old ideas of success and competition, and freely enter realms of innovation and genuine creativity.

The value of your gap is incalculable, even when you find yourself questioning it.

What Belongs and What Doesn't

The gap is its own cleanup detail. Whatever your path, and however you arrived there, the gap helps you sort through the stuff you have accumulated along the way. This process of taking inventory is important. Some of your stuff belongs, and some of it is bogging you down. The distinction is not always apparent. Some of the "right stuff" feels all wrong, and some of the "wrong stuff" makes you feel right at home.

The confusion stems from habitual points of view that crowd your path, even after they have outlived their usefulness. They made sense and created comfort in previous chapters of your life, but now they are slowing your progress. The gap will strip away these outdated mind-sets *if* you embrace the process. The *if* is consequential. You are the only one authorized to jettison excess baggage. Unless you make the call, stagnation could become the hallmark of your journey.

Schlepping old junk around is costly. The price is greatness itself. You heard me right—*greatness*. Something deep in our DNA beckons us to greatness. For many, the invitation is filed away, its promise buried by feelings of low self-worth, rejection, failure, and the fear of change. Success stories go unwritten; lives end unfulfilled.

This should not be. It is time to unearth the greatness.

The Antidote to Greatness

How many people do you suppose have felt the tug of entrepreneurship, for example? The answer is, *many*. Yet how many respond by laying it all on the line? The answer is, *very few*.

I realize how challenging such decisions are and how many factors must be considered. Financial viability and timing are valid considerations. So are family concerns. Yet not everyone who resists the tug does so for the right reasons. As a life coach, I have seen countless people struggle, not so much with legitimate considerations but with fear-based perceptions of those considerations.

The following fictitious example makes the distinction: Jeff is an experienced manager at Acme Manufacturing. He punches the clock faithfully and stays late when needed. He executes his responsibilities with precision. His proficiency strengthens the firm and provides his family with a good living. Every other Friday, his paycheck drops, and his bills are paid.

Jeff knows manufacturing and understands the widgets his company makes. He dreams about innovating Acme's product line, but his bosses show no interest in his ideas. His brother-in-law, Mike, is very interested. Experienced in business startups and armed with an understanding of the industry, Mike is willing to help Jeff, even to partner with him; but Jeff drags his feet.

Being an employee is all Jeff has ever known. The idea of going into business makes him uneasy. Meanwhile, his family believes his ideas are valuable and worth pursuing. They are able to sustain a period of uncertainty and are willing to make any adjustments the new opportunity might require. But Jeff perceives the downsides far more clearly than the potential benefits of starting something new.

Fast-forward ten years. The industry has caught up with Jeff's innovative ideas. Acme's main competitor, ABC Widgets, is lighting up the market with an idea Jeff envisioned long ago. Their plant turns out product twenty-four hours a day, and even so, they can barely meet demand. ABC's

CEO is earning a fortune and making a name for himself. The company's stock is soaring. The sales force is cashing in. The industry has been turned on its ear.

And where is Jeff? He's punching in at eight each morning for a company that has lost significant market share. Chances are, Acme will rebound. If they don't, the security Jeff savored ten years ago might vanish, despite his efforts to protect it. In the end, his biggest risk was the failure to clear away the self-limiting ideas that cluttered his path and caused him to decline the call of greatness. Deep down, he probably doubted that greatness was in his DNA to begin with. So, instead of focusing on his enormous potential, he majored on everything that could possibly go wrong.

When you know that you are beckoned to greatness, and you give yourself permission to agree, you can move past outdated, fear-based perceptions. Much of this progress is decided in the gap. There is no better place to discover what is already inside you.

> To what extent do you believe Jeff's choices were conscious? Have you seen others make similar choices?

Knowledge Without Wisdom

"What?" is a knowledge question. "How?" involves wisdom. For roughly seventy years, our culture has been driven by the pursuit of knowledge. The volume and rate of scientific advancement, and the societal transformations that have followed, are mind-boggling. Microchips, fiber optics, genetic medicine, lasers, and other innovations have redrawn our paradigms and revolutionized our expectations.

Do you remember when the Internet first became part of everyday conversation? The term *information superhighway* broke the ice and helped ordinary people understand the Internet's practical application to their lives. The idea soon went mainstream, and people everywhere began surfing the "net."

For a culture that craves knowledge, the crown jewel of information was a game-changer. Today, the Internet is at the fingertips of most Americans, wherever they go. With an online connection, a search engine, and a few clicks, anyone can learn about almost anything.

The craving for knowledge seems to be unlimited, so the Internet grows exponentially to satisfy demand. Its networks are predicted to "double in size every 5.32 years."[3] Its reach has branched beyond the business of information and into the business of commerce, the practice of medicine, and the execution of war. Today's consumer can purchase almost any product without leaving home. Doctors consult with patients on distant continents. Soldiers track and kill enemies from remote locations thousands of miles from any battlefield.

With this being the case, why do people with unrestricted access to virtual storehouses of knowledge still make bad decisions? Every day, news stories boggle our minds and shatter our trust in one another. We stand aghast at horrific crimes, cruel schemes, and lapses in leadership. We cringe as prominent people who seemed to have it all decide that "all" is not enough. We read their stories and wince at the damage they do.

Consider the downfall of "Wall Street wizard" Bernard Madoff. The financier amassed great wealth and enjoyed the respect of his industry. He had knowledge enough to create a vast personal empire. Yet, his career came crashing to an end when he used his knowledge to create a Ponzi scheme involving billions of dollars of other people's money. He knew the plan was illegal and that it jeopardized the innocent. He knew that he, his family, and his associates could be ruined and disgraced. But even knowing the risks was not enough to quench Madoff's compulsion for more money.

Knowledge is never enough. Without the wisdom to tell us *how* to apply our knowledge in ways that benefit ourselves, our fellow man, and society as a whole, even "good" knowledge can prove dangerous.

Busyness Versus Barrenness

As we consider other people's wisdom deficits, we must acknowledge that we have deficits of our own. The examples in these pages might not apply directly to our lives, but they shed light on the situations all people face.

Do you know any workaholics? You probably do, and they may be some of the smartest people around. Yet their workaholism is costing them and their families more than they probably realize. Their children long for attention. Their spouses feel abandoned. Their social lives are virtually extinct. They confuse *who they are* with *what they do*, and they wear themselves out trying to bolster their self-image.

Most workaholics live to regret their mistakes. Intellectually, they may realize that their lives are out of whack, but they lack the wherewithal to make a healthy change. They try to fix their problems by working harder, failing to understand that burnout is not the answer. Instead of gaining more of what they desire, their busyness leads to places of barrenness.

It can happen to the most well-intentioned people. You probably know someone who sports a "Mom's Taxi" bumper sticker on her SUV. She drives her kids to school in the morning and then shuttles them from one activity to another all afternoon and into the evening. Her son plays football and competes on the debate team. Her daughter plays soccer and sings in the school choir. A third child takes violin lessons and tutors younger kids in math.

Great moms will do almost anything to facilitate the positive pursuits of their children. But at what point does the family's busyness become barrenness? Is Mom's taxi service diverting her energy away from more fundamental responsibilities? Is she less aware of her son's insecurities or her daughter's struggle with self-worth? Have the children's crisscrossing schedules made conversation over dinner a thing of the past?

There is wisdom in balance. Being a couch potato is not the answer, but neither is spreading yourself too thin. So, get busy doing the things you love or that you need to do, but do it in such a way that you leave barrenness behind you.

Old Chapters, New Chapters, and the Rest of Your Life

Navigating the gap is a proactive pursuit. If you own it, the gap will develop within you a keener awareness of what your life is really about. It will help you find meaning in your past, joy in your present, and purpose in your future. It will let you know, in no uncertain terms, that chapters of life come and go. No season lasts forever, and living in the past never works.

If you are in your thirties, you have probably had to let go of the past more than once. You can likely remember wanting certain things in your teens and in your twenties that no longer hold any interest for you. You have outgrown certain desires and motivations. The same old people and ideas do not inspire you as they once did. You might not know how or why, but you sense that you have moved on. You can say without regret that you have been there, done that, and tossed the T-shirt in the ragbag.

Moving on is healthy. It shows that you welcome growth and desire a sustainable mode of living. You were not built to keep crossing the same bridge, climbing the same mountain, or passing through the same door for the rest of your life. You have new bridges ahead, higher mountains to conquer, and surprising new portals to enter. In a perfect world, you know this to be true, and you live it every day. However, there is no perfect world, and there is always more to learn.

As a life coach, part of my job is to draw people toward truth and objectivity so they can articulate their feelings and see past them. One of the mainstays of coaching is to ask questions. The right questions can cause a monochromatic worldview to "pop" with fresh color and a renewed sense of reality. The questions I like to ask often sound simplistic, yet they expose hidden thought patterns and give my clients the freedom to change their minds in conscious and constructive ways.

Below, I have listed some of the questions I commonly use. Ask them of yourself the way a coach would ask them—with intentionality and with a desire to spark new realms of conversation. Take time to push past "the usual" answers until you understand what is underneath them. Allow one question to lead to another, and you will discover things you never knew—*about yourself*!

You have heard the first question already. Now you get to answer it.

- What are you doing the rest of your life? (If you assume that it is the same thing you're doing right now, you need to push the envelope and think again!)

- What will it take for you to build a more sustainable, effective, and productive lifestyle? (Life is never about arriving but about creating a path *to* and *for* your future. What might that path look like?)

- Which specific accomplishments (personal and professional) continue to elude you? (Documenting this inventory will help you update your desires and understand the meaning behind them.)

- Which areas of your heart need to line up with the quality of life you desire? (Unless you look within, you will remain unaware of self-sabotaging tendencies. Don't be afraid to discover the culprits.)

- Which parts of your soul feel broken and in need of restoration? (How might emotional wounds, pain, or loss be stifling your ability to dream and hope for a promising future? How have past outcomes capped your future expectations?)

- Right now, what do you desire more than anything else? (Be specific and make sure your answer is current. Too often, we try to resurrect desires from previous chapters of our lives. We sometimes do this because we have not allowed ourselves to consider new dreams.)

The dreams sleeping inside you can be awakened. They are worthy of being awakened, because you are worthy of their promise. So, go ahead and own them!

The Coach in Your Pocket

Everyone stands to benefit from a relationship with a life coach. A book like this one—what I call the "coach in your pocket"—can go with you anywhere, anytime. It was written to help you process information and extract wisdom that is applicable to *your* life. If you will drill down into what you read, you will glean from powerful, time-tested coaching principles that have changed lives, and you will be able to do so at your own pace.

When coaching is taken to heart, it is more transformative than you might imagine. Life coaching is, above all, a conversation. Many of us have similar conversations with mentors, employers, pastors, siblings, and parents. Some of these exchanges are informal and even random, while others, such as the mentor/mentee relationship, are more carefully directed and goal-oriented.

This book is based specifically on the coaching relationship—a specific kind of conversation involving mutual intent and understanding of what the experience is meant to accomplish. The conversation occurs in a safe environment from which you can explore and implement new ways of thinking about, perceiving, and pursuing goals.

All you need now is your official invitation.

You Are Invited!

At the heart of the coaching conversation is an invitation to make a promise. You are invited to embrace change and to take specific actions in keeping with your stated goals. This promise keeps the conversation productive. Everyone wants a better life, but *wanting* it is not enough. *Having* it requires a commitment to follow through. In the end, only you can keep this promise.

You can see that success rests largely on your willingness to deliver. Without your commitment, even the best life coach cannot help. It is your actions that must create a climate conducive to change. Your attitude is equally important. For coaching to bear fruit in your life, you'll need to embrace the discomfort that transparency often brings. How else can you expect to discover and dismantle hidden structures that have been holding you back? (We will uncover these structures in coming chapters. You will see how comfortable yet counterproductive they are, and you will break free from them.)

Coaches and sound coaching principles also play a role in good outcomes. Part of the process is to discern people's underlying needs and to challenge their perceptions. More often than not, clients unconsciously protect their misperceptions, which often involve their abilities, capacities, and competencies. For example, an aspiring singer may come to the coaching conversation completely unaware that he or she is tone-deaf. Friends and loved ones may have avoided breaking the news for fear of hurting the "singer's" feelings.

Coaches do not enjoy such luxuries as white lies; the conversation must be truthful. Sugarcoating the truth only dumps people onto dead-end paths. That kind of help is no help at all. Of course, not all clients overestimate their gifts. Some are self-deprecating and dismissive of their abilities. They need help discovering their talents, acknowledging or owning them, and putting them to use. Good coaching helps people to see themselves objectively and to frame achievable goals based on an accurate self-perception.

The "coach in your pocket" can take you only as far as you are willing to go. You must decide how far that is, and determine that you will make choices consistent with what's needed to reach your destination.

What's on Your Agenda?

People seek the services of life coaches for almost as many reasons as there are people. Some of the most universal goals that prompt people to hire a life coach, each of which I will explore briefly below, are money; a balanced life; effective, connective communication; the elimination of energy-drainers; healthy relationships; meaning; stress relief; and skill development. Consider these goals to be part of the coaching conversation now under way in your life. A word of caution: The fact that these goals are so common may tempt you to gloss over them. My advice is, *don't*.

This is your journey, and you get only one. Take the time to ask yourself how these issues apply (or don't apply) in your situation. Consider what growth would look like in your case. Finally, ask yourself which of these issues are with you in the gap. You may be surprised at what you learn.

Money

Most people think a lot about money. In today's challenging global climate, the preoccupation is more widespread. People who once believed they were financially secure are losing confidence and tightening their belts. Many want to curb spending without sacrificing the lifestyles to which they have grown accustomed. The search for ways to do this often leads to new, more creative methods of achieving personal and professional goals.

Financial concerns are important, because cash flow affects the way your life flows. Money can facilitate the realization of dreams, support better health, and help the needy, whereas financial lack can keep your dreams on hold, compromise healthful choices, and keep you on the receiving end of charity.

Many coaching clients want to change their outcomes where money is concerned. Some of them need to pivot in response to the current financial environment. Others want to break longstanding patterns of loss and lack. Still others want to find innovative ways of financing their dreams.

A Balanced Life

For many people, the rapid pace of modern society makes it difficult to a life of order and balance. High degrees of uncertainty, a decreasing sense of security, and the demands of juggling a myriad of priorities make harmony difficult to achieve. Many coaching clients suffer from a lack of focus and clear direction. They want to simplify their lives, undo their disorientation, and detect and eliminate any blind spots that are contributing to their sense of imbalance, all in an effort to achieve a less stressful, more peaceful way of life.

Effective, Connective Communication

Words are said to create worlds. As fundamental elements of our thinking and communicating, words frame our life environments. Many coaching clients live with the damage caused by troubled communications. They are aware of the consequences in their homes and careers, and they want to understand how their interactions produced those results, so that they can prevent the cycle from continuing. They are also seeking more productive ways of communicating in the hope of producing better outcomes in the future.

Life coaches often help clients learn to listen and respond in ways that build rapport with others. Effective communicators not only enjoy better relationships but also benefit in their professional lives, as well, with the result being better networks and even higher profits.

Elimination of Energy-Drainers

An energy-drainer is any activity or circumstance that depletes your physical, emotional, mental, and spiritual energy, or decreases your motivation to take care of yourself. Energy is drained in more ways than we have space to discuss here, but you can probably identify some of your signature energy-drainers!

Whether you are dealing with demands for increased productivity on the job, soaring inflation, or a challenging business environment, you can feel as though you are losing control. You may be so weighed down, physically and emotionally, that you wake up exhausted every morning.

Many who seek coaching say they want to get their lives back. They don't always know what that will look like, but they know that something has to change. An effective life coach understands the need for structures to help them sustain motivation, improve physical energy, and develop a healthy sense of ambition.

Healthy Relationships

In every century, relationships have been front and center. Relationships function within common *social containers*. One of the most important social containers is the family, which includes other containers, such as the couple container, the parent container, and the grandparent container. Not all social containers involve relatives, of course. Professional containers include the often complex systems and networks of relationships in which we interact daily in order to do our jobs.

Whatever the context, relationships are central to life. People today feel the effects of our high-tech culture and are crying out for *high-touch* relationships—not in the physical sense, but in the deeper sense that counters the superficial interaction that is so prevalent. Becoming more intimate with loved ones, more honoring of friends, and more connected with coworkers are high on most people's agendas.

Meaning

The crisis of meaning, which we already discussed to a degree, is perhaps the single most enduring crisis of our time. People are seeking meaning in their present situations and ultimate concerns, often with a spiritual bent to their search. Many find themselves questioning their personal vision, mission, and purpose. The self-absorbed, materialistic bent of modern society has left them feeling empty and looking for more substantial quests. Often, the famine of meaning leads them to desire intimacy with their Maker and with their fellow man. Every coaching conversation involves meaning, on some level.

Stress Relief

Many individuals seek coaching because a loved one, employer, advisory board, or board of directors has required them to do so. These requests are usually made in the hopes that the individual can find effective ways to de-stress. He or she may be a workaholic "alpha leader" who has fallen into the pattern of "all work and no play" that is so harmful to life, health, and professional effectiveness. Life coaches can help clients identify and uproot the causes of workaholism and establish healthier lifestyles.

Skill Development

Many coaching clients simply want to refine and upgrade their skill sets and pursue higher levels of achievement. They may be accustomed to significant levels of success but are looking to raise their game. Some are entrepreneurs who want to build thriving enterprises, enhance sales potential, and increase profitability. Others work in the corporate world and want to ensure their company's long-term sustainability. Some want to write the next best-selling novel or "how-to" book. Whatever the enterprise, these clients are motivated by new prospects.

> Which of these universal agenda items resonates most closely with you? Does it surprise you, or not? Are there any insights to glean from your reaction?

Everyone Needs Navigational Assistance

Whether you are a twenty-something eager to explore untested dreams or a sixty-something going on forty and ready to reinvent yourself, the coaching principles in the coming chapters will fuel your fire and cast revelatory light on the road ahead.

Your path is one of a kind and contains valuable clues. Some are easy to detect and understand. Others are so hidden that you do not see them yet. *But you will.* You were born a meaning-maker, created to draw significance from even the most inscrutable situations.

So, congratulations! This is your grand opportunity to break the meaning of your life wide-open. Your gap—the "nowhere" between two "somewheres"—is calling, and the coach in your pocket is here to help.

Let's pull up anchor and start navigating!

Sounding the Depths

1. Which components of your current path give you comfort? Which are cooperating with your destination, and which do you suspect are blocking your progress? How so?

2. Describe your reaction to the hypothetical story I shared about Jeff. What questions might a life coach ask you about your reaction? What do your answers reveal about your own journey?

3. Where has your busyness produced barrenness? Which assumptions might have coaxed you in this direction? How are these assumptions valid or invalid? How might wisdom reframe your approach?

4. What kinds of questions about your life make you uncomfortable? Explain how your reactions might be flagging "old" things that you are trying to protect.

5. How will you use the "coach in your pocket"? What previous coaching have you pursued? How will you approach this experience differently in the future?

Notes

1. Music by Michel Legrand, lyrics by Alan and Marilyn Bergman, 1969, United Artists Music Co., Inc.; EMI Catalog, Inc.; Warner Brothers Publications.
2. http://www.goodreads.com/author/quotes/20105.Joseph_Campbell.
3. Lisa Zyga, "Internet Growth Follows Moore's Law Too," PhysOrg.com, http://phys.org/news151162452.html.

2

The Nowhere Between
Two Somewheres

Imagine this scenario: Your family piles into the SUV for the mother of all road trips. Snacks are packed. Bottled water is on ice. The kids are pumped up. Your spouse is more than ready to unwind. You've spent months planning your journey and printing out directions to the scenic routes you know will create great memories and offer great photo ops. Now, finally, it's time to roll. Your destination beckons, and the road unfurls before you like a red carpet to adventure.

You planned some surprises, but getting lost was not one of them. With your GPS backing you up, going off course barely seems possible. Then, without warning, the paved road turns to gravel...then dirt...and then to thick brush. You are in a state you know nothing about with a population one third that of the city in which you live. Twenty miles separate the closest neighbors here, and even if you could bring yourself to ask for directions, there isn't a soul in sight.

The once-reassuring voice of your GPS now raises your ire as it recommends taking the first available U-turn. You're positive that driving into a wooded knoll is a bad idea. You should have known something was up when you first heard gravel crunching under your wheels. Now, your "knower" is on overload. You have entered some kind of nowhere, and you need to get your bearings.

So, you shift into reverse and follow the brush back to the dirt… and then the gravel…and finally back to your scenic route. You look for the rest stop you passed before the pavement ran out. It looked like nothing when you first saw it. No gas station. No fast food. No souvenir shop. Nothing.

But it is a place to regroup, and it has a restroom. Even more important is the worn wooden sign with a faded red arrow, beside which is posted the information you need. It is precious little when your current reality feels like nowhere, yet the words "You are here" are a start—a very, very good start.

This Is like Nowhere, Man

Knowing "you are here" is helpful, even when you land in a "nowhere" between two "somewheres," as John Lennon did in the mid-sixties. His experience was memorialized in the song "Nowhere Man" from the Beatles' verging-on-psychedelic album *Rubber Soul*. The single's title and its melancholy musical strains captured the frustrating and virtually universal experience of a man making plans without purpose.

Half a decade after the song's release, *Rolling Stone* magazine founder Jann Wenner interviewed Lennon and asked him who the song was about. Lennon's answer sounds like the journal entry of a seasoned gap navigator:

> Probably about myself. I remember I was just going through this paranoia trying to write something and nothing would come out, so I just lay down and tried to not write and then this came out, the whole thing came out in one gulp.[3]

Lennon was one half of a history-making songwriting team, yet he was stuck—and he knew it. He was lodged in a nowhere place where even his creativity failed him. He tried to find the words but came up empty. The creative process he knew so well was just not working.

As lost as he felt, Lennon remained self-aware and conscious of his surroundings. He was obviously in a place that was new and different, and so, instead of trying to force the issue, he chose to simply adjust to it.

The world-class songwriter humbled himself and tried something completely counterintuitive: *not writing*. Suddenly, the logjam broke, and the song seemed to write itself! The struggle gave way to a missive that mirrored Lennon's experience. But it was not all about him. Everyone who heard the song *got it*. They had either visited "Nowhere Land" or knew someone who had. And as millions embraced the message, Lennon's bank account grew. Decades later, even his handwritten song notes brought nearly half a million dollars at auction![2]

Lennon found the red arrow. It said that he was stuck in a nowhere place, but even his nowhere was worth something.

So is yours. Explore it! Yes, the gap is often uncomfortable. But you can make the place work for you. You just might find a new road, a novel source, or the destiny opportunity you never thought you'd see.

> Are you feeling *nowhere*? What might you manage to glean from this place? A new idea? A fresh perspective? A better sense of who you are?

What Is Your Red Arrow Saying?

Finding that red arrow is your first job in the gap. Regardless of how your current reality looks, it is imperative to recognize it for what it is. Don't waste your energy dressing it up or denying its downsides. Just accept that you're *here* and stay focused on where you are going. You absolutely cannot reach the latter until you have faced the former.

As you read that last sentence, did you nod in agreement and then scan ahead for the "real" point?

"Slow down," says your pocket coach. "That *was* the real point."

I cannot stress it enough: Millions of people believe they understand their current reality when they really don't. The more familiar the place becomes, the less they really see it, and the more they miss its meaning. The more painful the place is, the more rationales they create to explain it away and bury what they refuse to see.

Familiarity creates a form of blindness, so that we mentally assent to features in our paradigms without digesting their meaning. This rote agreement is more habitual than we realize. We think that because we recognize familiar places or ideas and even repeatedly affirm them, that we have also processed and internalized them.

Not necessarily! Millions of people are familiar with the eighth of the Ten Commandments: *"Thou shalt not steal"* (Exodus 20:15). They nod at the words, leaving little doubt that they agree with the principle. When they hear about a thief being apprehended, they are quick to say, "Lock up that bum and throw away the key!"

Their moral outrage affirms their stance, yet they fudge and finagle their tax returns year after year. They have mentally assented to the idea that stealing is wrong, but they are not yet living in accordance with it. There is a disconnect between where they think their red arrow is and its actual location.

For the record, we are always in the process of reconciling our sense of current reality with the reality that actually is. Yet we don't always do it voluntarily. For some, the wake-up call comes when IRS agents show up at the door. But, one way or another, we continually find pieces of our current reality hidden in our blind spots.

There is no better place than the gap for getting this job done. Of course, the process doesn't go only one way—you can misunderstand your best features just as easily as you can your less appealing ones. You might be a diligent employee, doing your best each and every day. Yet, when your boss compliments your work, you may respond as though you are undeserving of the attention.

It happens all the time. Why? Because there is a difference between where we are and where we *think* we are. Even when our performance is excellent, our sense of self-worth can be fractured. We mistakenly believe that everyone else is smarter, better, or more skilled than we are.

How often and how easily we deceive ourselves—and how important the gap is in helping us to realize it! Friend, you might feel like you are flailing and getting nowhere, but you are on your way to somewhere. Your red arrow will help you to see your current reality as it actually is, if you are willing to allow it to.

Unwelcome Reality

This coaching conversation will help you ferret out any wrong assumptions about your current reality and establish honest baselines so you know exactly where you are. But let me warn you: When you slap that red arrow dead center on your actual current reality, it is often a startling experience sure to stir your emotions.

It is a mountaintop and a valley experience in one. Few things will make you feel better than leaving the old misperceptions behind. But doing so also lays bare the boundaries of your comfort zone. With the fig leaves peeled off and your current reality exposed, you can expect to feel the sting.

Even when your red arrow hints of promise, your current reality, by definition, falls short of your ultimate vision. This is part of the gap experience, and there are plenty of emotions attached to it. At times, you will be tempted to flee the "classroom" and stifle the truths you uncovered there. Without realizing it, you may rationalize the experience and make excuses for the shape you are in.

You have probably heard about people with wallets full of maxed-out credit cards. You may be in that situation now. You may have told yourself, in all earnestness, "I'll get my finances under control next year. If I can tread water a little longer and maintain my minimum payments for a few more months, I'll make that big sale/get that promotion/etc. Then I can wipe the debt clean in one easy shot."

You might very well make that sale or get that promotion. I hope you do! But what if you don't? Or what if the timing isn't right? Your current reality may be more volatile than you realize. If your credit cards are maxed out, you are sitting on a powder keg of interest and fees that are accruing faster than your income is growing. Your desired reality (hitting your financial stride and paying off your cards) is well-meaning, but unless it is based on an accurate assessment of where you are and how fast your reality can change, you are deluding yourself, and you have less control over the situation than you think.

The objective reality looks more like this: You are drowning in debt and very well might reach a tipping point before your financial goals are met. When the banks realize that you are in trouble, they will raise your interest rates. The minimum payments you thought were manageable will get quickly out of hand. The banks will have you over a barrel, and not the other way around. If they call in their markers, whatever control you thought you had will evaporate.

Your dream of paying up when your desired reality kicks in could turn out to be a fantasy—not because you are looking to default, but because you assessed your level of control according to where you *thought* you were. To achieve your goals and reach your stated destination, you must understand and accept where you *really* are. Whether good, bad, or really ugly, the truth is your only starting point.

Gap Assessment

In the coaching world, the *gap* (the nowhere between two somewheres) is the distance between your current reality (where you are) and your desired reality (where you want to be). That sounds simple enough—and it is, when your measurements are right. But when your sense of current reality is skewed, and your desired destination is farther off than you think, life gets complicated.

Destination matters, but so does distance. Any traveler knows that. So, let's plan a virtual trip. Suppose that you are vacationing with friends in Portland, Maine, after which you must drive to New York City for a job interview. You know that if you nail your presentation, you will secure the career of your dreams. So, you plan carefully and allow plenty of time for the drive. You plan to leave Portland at night, knock off a chunk of your trip, and check in to a hotel just outside Boston. After a good night's sleep, you will finish your run to the Big Apple.

You leave your friends and head for Boston. You are not terribly familiar with the route from Portland, but it is a straight run and should pose no problems. You crank the stereo and sip some coffee. Sooner than expected, you arrive on the outskirts of Beantown. You grab a hotel room and set your alarm for 6 A.M.

You are very familiar with the second leg of the drive. You know how far it is from Boston to New York City and what the speed limits are. You have alternate routes in mind, in case you come upon road work or a traffic accident. You allow one hour for a shower and breakfast, plus five hours travel time, just in case. Your plan seems bulletproof. You are relaxed and ready to meet your interviewers. Your contact at the firm in New York confirms your 11 AM appointment. Everything is falling into place.

There is only one problem: You are not just outside Boston, as you assumed. You actually spent the night closer to Portsmouth, Maine. Instead of driving 210 miles to your interview, you will have to cover 270 miles.

Had you accurately assessed your starting point, you could have adjusted your plans. You might have set your alarm for 5 AM and grabbed breakfast on the fly. As it stands, your opportunity is in jeopardy. You might show up late to your appointment and destroy the good impression you had hoped to make. At best, your interview could be compromised. At worst, your dream could be, too.

A distance of sixty miles has become a very big deal. Instead of feeling cool, calm, and collected, you feel your stress mounting. The distance between your current reality and your desired reality is greater than you thought. If you blow this interview, the gap could get even bigger.

When it comes to gaps, distance matters.

> Does this story sound like a bad dream, or even a nightmare? Have you ever had such a dream? Are you living one right now?

Denial Equals Delay

You can see that making an accurate assessment of your gap is more important than you might sometimes realize. If we are honest, we must admit that we often misjudge the gap we're in. Sometimes, we allow time constraints and misplaced priorities to rush our measurements. At other times, we simply deny the size of the gap, hoping to cover over our stagnant places and our missteps.

These attempts to cover up our gap are based in shame. Because we fear humiliation, we make desperate and even dangerous choices, and develop tremendous capacities for living in denial. We hope against hope that the issues we ignore will go away and never return. Instead, everything we try to bury stays alive. What we refuse to deal with today resurfaces tomorrow. Our cover-ups delay our consequences; worse, they also exacerbate them.

If you sincerely desire to close the gap between where you are and where you want to be, you must deal with the facts as they are, not as you wish they were. That is why making an honest, accurate assessment of your current reality is absolutely nonnegotiable.

Such honesty and transparency might be new to you, not because you aim to be deceptive, but because you believe that the presence of pain is proof of failure. Adjust your thinking and look your pain in the eye. Expect some resistance as you transition out of denial, but don't quit. Just admit where you are, and then take your next step.

Denial in a Society of Self-admiration

Have you noticed the modern tendency to focus on *self*? Even the people who believe that humans evolved from apes promote self-admiration and humanistic thought. The word *hero* is overused, cheapening true acts of valor. Medical professionals acting under oath to preserve life are commended for having the "courage" to kill innocents in the womb. An increasingly widespread mind-set that life is one big party, and the glorification of celebrities, are contributing to a general disdain for personal responsibility.

It is no wonder that denial is so prevalent. It has found the perfect climate in which to grow! Society thrives on the denial of current reality and, as a result, fails to address the systemic problems plaguing the population at the root. We excuse destructive societal patterns—family breakdowns, unethical leadership, entitlement mind-sets, and the loss of respect of life—or suggest superficial fixes. Instead of shedding light on the truth, we try to deemphasize it in order to avoid "offending" anyone.

Society cannot change for the better until we are willing to face our current reality, individually and corporately. If societal wholeness is our purpose, we must deal with root issues and refuse to concoct excuses. Ultimately, we must release our grip on what we claim not to want *before* we can lay hold of what we say we desire.

Again, whatever we try to bury stays alive and continues to affect us. We must decide what belongs on our societal path and what doesn't. That means uncovering what is there and dealing with it at the root.

> Self-admiration has created a culture of narcissism and a "love gap" that diminishes us. What the world needs most is a love that is the polar opposite of narcissism. A love that is selfless and self-abandoning. A love that does not ask, "What's in it for me?" but "What's in it for those I am privileged to know?" A love that isn't about being served but serving others. Your dreams come alive when you are preoccupied with making other people's dreams come true. That is where real happiness is found.

Structures and Gaps

Earlier, we touched on social containers, such as our immediate and extended families, workplaces and related networks, church groups, and other relational structures. Just as social structures help build society, inner structures frame our individual lives. We will soon discover how these structures work. Right now, we need to realize that they exist, and learn how to recognize them.

Structure is essential to all function, and everything has a structure—current reality included. Composer, filmmaker, and organizational consultant Robert Fritz articulated structure in such a way that serves as a good place for us to start:

Structure is a whole thing. A car is a structure. A rocking chair is a structure. A building is a structure, as is the human body. A structure is an entity that is undivided, complete and total.[3]

Structures are everywhere. Your brain is a structure. So is your home. Your workplace is a structure. So is your garage door. On a broader scale, molecular structures form when atoms bind together. Economic structures facilitate commerce and governance. Soil structure is tied to ecology and agriculture. Planes, trains, automobiles, and spaceships are structured for movement in various environments.

A structure's design is inseparable from its function. The most brilliantly designed tractor would not serve the needs of a suburban commuter because farm vehicles are not designed for highway use. Cars are built for that. They are aerodynamic, their suspension provides a smooth ride, they are easy to get in and out of, and they fit into the average parking space.

The connection between structure and function is critical. When it is compromised, functionality is lost, and structures fail. This is not only true of technology; it also applies to your life structures. For instance, your personality is a structure that is important to your purpose and your relationships. When it is damaged by trauma, for example, your purpose is thwarted, your relationships adversely affected. Another example: Your belief systems are structures that provide guidance and meaning. When they are skewed by deception, you may misunderstand where you fit in the world and how it works.

Structures are fully understood only from the inside out. Your external life is governed by internal structures. If you are familiar with these structures and you understand them, your outcomes will make sense to you. You will see that wherever your life functions well and yields positive outcomes, your structure is aligned with your purpose. And where outcomes are consistently troublesome, you will know that a structure (or structures) is contradicting your purpose.

How do you locate these contrary structures? Just pay attention to your frustrations. Where frustration shows up—especially repeatedly—structure is almost certainly opposing purpose. Is your home life frustrating? Then follow the frustration to its source. If the problem is strife, find its supporting structures. It may be a belief system that formed when your parents' marriage failed or when your spouse was abandoned at an early age. There may be codependent tendencies or other issues complicating your family dynamics.

Do you see how structures can work against your purpose in life? This part of our coaching conversation is not meant to take potshots at your broken places. Everyone has them! The intent here is to create an awareness of structures so that you can begin to consciously align them with your purpose by asking yourself, "How is life working for me?"

You might feel stuck in a pattern of one step forward, two steps back. You might be recycling what you don't want instead of moving toward what you do. Maybe you wonder about your choices; perhaps you regret a decision so bad, you still cannot explain why you made it. Whatever the issue, it is governed by layers of structures within your heart and mind. In coming chapters, you will learn more about these structures as we explore them, layer by layer, so that you may rebuild, restore, or reject them, as the case may be.

In the meantime, rest assured that your gap—your nowhere between two somewhere—is an important place and a normal part of the human journey. Believe it or not, it is a very beautiful chapter in the life story you have been writing all these years.

Sounding the Depths

1. How might you respond more constructively to a "nowhere place" in your life?

2. Where is your red arrow, and what is it telling you? How does its message compare with your initial understanding of your current reality?

3. Are you aware of any areas in which you have been using the mechanism of denial? What is it costing you?

4. Identify one area of denial in today's society. How does it affect your life? How will it affect the next generation if left unchecked?

5. Had you previously assumed that the structures in your life are static? Has your mind changed? How so?

Notes

1. Jann S. Wenner et al., *The Rolling Stone Interviews, 1967–1980: Talking with the Legends of Rock & Roll* (New York: St. Martin's Press, 1981), 148.

2. "Handwritten Lennon Song Auctioned," BBC News Online, November 19, 2003, http://news.bbc.co.uk/2/hi/entertainment/3282991.stm.

3. "Principles," Robert Fritz, Inc., http://www.robertfritz.com/index.php?content=principles.

3

Your Journey, Your Story

If you are a baby boomer like me, you probably remember a television program called *This Is Your Life*. Every week, the host would devise a ruse to bring an unsuspecting and well-known featured guest together with a group of people he or she knew. The group often included childhood friends, coworkers, and loved ones, who then shared personal anecdotes and obscure facts about the individual's life.

The "inside information" kept viewers tuning in week after week, as the often humorous and sometimes tearful accounts revealed what newspapers and celebrity magazines rarely did. Stories about the honoree that showed his or her generosity, penchant for practical jokes, or early career mishaps helped the audience see him or her not as a luminary on a pedestal but a fellow human being on the journey called *life*.

Whether you live in fame or obscurity, you have a unique story and a journey unlike anyone else's. It is funny and sad, serious and lighthearted, complicated and easy to grasp. Some of your story is easy to know: You were born on a specific day. You attended certain schools. You pursued a particular line of work. Other elements of your story are less obvious and must be drawn out from deeper places before they can be understood and appreciated.

As you have seen, the coaching conversation draws out the parts of your story that operate undetected—though no less powerfully—from your inner landscape. As we go deeper, you will see much more of that process, and you will discover amazing things about the story you are writing.

The Reflection That Speaks

More and more, you are seeing how your life reflects what you believe and expect. So, it becomes necessary to ask, *What do you believe, and what do you expect?* Do you see your life as an experiment that you are conducting and expect to turn out well? Or do you see it as an undifferentiated blob of events that occur without your permission? Are you confident of your role in your story's development? Or do you feel like an accidental character written into a secret script by an indifferent playwright?

To answer this question, you might need to move past the beliefs and expectations crowding the top of your mind and dig through the ones that are incubating deep inside. The effort will be well worth it, because what you believe at the very deepest levels of your heart and mind is what you will live. If you believe you are the confident conductor of your life "experiment," that is what you will be. If you feel as if you're trapped inside a life of someone else's design, *that* will be your experience. Your life can be nothing more or less than what you believe.

Your life is no accident, and you have more power to shape it than you probably realize. At times, you may wonder where it is going or why. You may question its message or feel convinced that you were handed someone else's story by mistake. But if you are attentive, your story will speak clearly, revealing the enormous part you have played—and are still playing—in writing it. Every scene will parade an amazing design and explain what animates your outcomes. Your story will tell you that it is truly and wonderfully yours.

Your story, your own personal narrative, is unfolding even when you are unconscious of it. The events are unfolding where others can watch and participate. But the real story starts deep inside, where your thoughts, beliefs, and feelings live.

In Latin, to *narrate* means "to recount." According to the dictionary, a *narrative* is a story or account that is narrated, or an artistic representation of such a story.[1] Every narrative has a voice. What is yours saying?

Observer and Observed, and More

Your story shares a curious quality that you also experience when you dream. Think about a recent dream you had. You will notice that, although you were *in* the dream, you also *observed* it. In other words, you were both actor and audience. You may have experienced this phenomenon in certain waking moments, too—maybe as you "popped the question" to your future bride or had a close call on the highway.

People often describe experiences such as these with comments like, "It was as if I was watching a movie—and I was in it!" The phenomenon is more commonplace than you might realize. In the story of your life, you are both the observer and the observed. If your life were an actual movie, you would be the lead actor, as well as the writer, director, and producer!

The idea that you play such a big part in orchestrating your own journey might alarm you, especially if you have always believed that God is in control. Most Christians have been taught that God controls everything. The truth is, *He doesn't.* God never handed you a script and asked you to memorize it. He has not directed you to follow its every cue. You might believe that He has, but He hasn't. This belief is skewed just enough to mess with your story—and with His.

God made you in His image and likeness. (See Genesis 1:26–27.) You are a creative being, and He intends for you to use your creativity—not just to write your memoir someday, but to write your script as you live it out! You are not a puppet but a person with free will. You were not designed for passivity but for active engagement.

God created you with the capacity to *invoke, evoke,* and *provoke* your destiny. Invoking and evoking have to do with calling your destiny into being. This is not as ethereal as it might sound. It means bringing your purpose to mind and using your imagination to unfold, in your thought-life, things that will eventually happen, largely *because you thought about them.*

To provoke your destiny is to participate in ways that facilitate its fulfill-ment. If you envision a career in politics, you will work toward this destiny by studying history and keeping up with current issues. You might choose to pursue a law degree to bolster your understanding of our nation's legal sys-tem. Serving at the local level will help to develop your resume. Volunteering to help established political leaders will give you insight into what is next.

Whatever you do, you will do it by choice, as an act of your own will. That does not mean there is no God or that God is not involved in your life story. It means that what becomes of the story is in your hands. Two well-known Bible accounts reveal this truth. In the first, God told Adam to name the animals. (See Genesis 2:19–20.) He knew Adam's choices would have very long-term implications, and yet He gave him complete freedom in naming the creatures *He* had created. Adam helped to write God's story, as well as his own!

The story of the fall of man in the garden of Eden also proves that Adam was not bound to a script. (See Genesis 3.) Neither was his wife, Eve. Both of them chose the serpent's suggestion to eat the forbidden fruit over God's admonition not to eat it. If they had been bound to cues in God's "divine drama," they would have kicked the serpent out of the gar-den before he could get a word in edgewise.

If God wrote our "scripts," they would all be good ones, and they would benefit everyone involved. But they would still be controlling, and that is not His way. God gave Adam and Eve the power to write their own story, and they did.

He gave the same power to you.

Own Your Story—All of It

Early in this chapter, I asked you whether you believed your life was unfolding without your approval, against your intentions. If you answered in the affirmative, it means you believe that your life is out of your hands and in the control of someone or something else.

This perspective has significant consequences. If you believe that everything that happens between the moment of your birth and the hour of your death is thrust upon you by other people, by events outside of your control, or by other circumstances, you will unconsciously put yourself at the mercy of these forces and proclaim yourself their victim.

Truth be told, some events *are* beyond your control. So are the decisions of others. You cannot control the weather, political elections, or the economy. Nor can you control other people's choices. But when it comes to your own life, you have more control than anyone else. Only you can control the choices you make.

Those who see themselves as powerless in life rarely take ownership of their stories, for what would be their incentive to set priorities, express their deepest desires, determine their outcomes, or find their purpose? Once someone becomes convinced that his life is out of his hands, there is no such incentive. He thus forfeits his personal power, thereby guaranteeing himself more of what he has already experienced—downward spirals and nasty surprises.

Are you living this way? Does the realization come as a shock? Well, here is some great news: You still have the power to own your story. Of course, whether you own it or not, you will still write the script; why not do it consciously and *really live?*

Like all stories, yours includes a protagonist, a cast of secondary characters, a plot, a setting, a theme, a point of view, and a storyteller. Your decision to take ownership affects your whole story and touches many more lives than yours alone. The direction your life takes will affect other people's stories. Where your life goes affects other people's stories, so it's important to pay attention to the ways in which the other characters in your story (your loved ones, friends, coworkers, and so forth) share in your setting and impact the plot as they interact with you. What kind of setting is it? Does it support health or dangerous habits? Does it inspire big dreams, or a sense of dependency?

As you compose the theme of your story, are you encouraging them to take ownership of theirs?

Stories are essential to every culture. In ancient times, stories and myths were passed down to succeeding generations, either orally or written on parchment. These narratives connected individuals to the larger community, its history, and its worldview. Can you identify any stories or myths that inform your perspective?

Own the Freedom to Fail

We are quick to own our successes, but we need to own our failures, too. Even more important, we need to own the freedom to fail. Until we do, we cannot enjoy the freedom to turn our failures around.

As much as we dislike having other people tell us what to do and how to live, many of us also dislike taking responsibility and deciding these matters for ourselves. The problem is fear—fear of messing up; fear of being held accountable when things go wrong. We know that once we accept responsibility, we cannot point the finger elsewhere when life looks upside-down.

Because we are so afraid to fail, we take extreme measures to protect against and even eliminate the possibility of failure. There is only one way to do this "successfully," and that is to *avoid all risk*. That might sound like a good deal. Who wouldn't want a risk-free life? But that is not life at all; it is a form of death in which every opportunity to succeed dies on the vine.

Can you see how devastating and delusional this choice is? Yet millions of people, whether consciously or unconsciously, choose its anesthetizing effects. In exchange for a sense of security (however false) and the avoidance of difficult (yet potentially powerful) decisions, they sacrifice their ability to soar.

You cannot live the life you long for unless you are willing to fail. In fact, you cannot succeed until you give yourself *permission* to fail. Everyone who has achieved great things in any field has accepted this reality. It doesn't mean they did not fear failure; it simply means they succeeded anyway.

When I was a kid growing up in New York City, there was no bigger name than Mickey Mantle. I believed the guy walked on water, and I was partly right: Mantle ranks sixteenth on the list of home run hitters in Major League Baseball history. Sitting behind home plate, I watched The Mick's switch-hitting genius. Whichever side of the rubber he stood on, he visited dread upon his opponents.

When people reminisce about Mickey Mantle, they rarely mention his 1,710 strikeouts.[2] They talk about his 536 homers[3] and the sound of his bat connecting with the sweet spot on the ball. They can still hear the fierce c-r-a-c-k that told them it was headed out of the park.

Mantle did not homer every at bat, or even every game. But, regardless of what he did at the plate, he accomplished his mission. He succeeded because he gave himself permission to fail. He was willing to swing and miss, and he did plenty of that. The idea of racking up 1,710 strikeouts might have scared off other guys, but not Mantle. He knew he could not hit home runs without swinging big.

Strikeouts were a necessary part of Mickey Mantle's journey. I'm sure he hated being beaten by a pitch, and I know my heart sank every time he was. But every strike gave him the feedback he needed to become a better hitter with a better story, for him and for his team.

Inside Your Story

We have talked about some of the outward elements of your story, including characters, setting, plot, and so forth. But wrapped up inside your story are other, less conspicuous, parts that are just as important and even more fundamental to the story you end up writing.

Beliefs

What you believe underlies all that you say and do. This is a powerful statement, so be sure you take it in. You cannot act, make choices, or do anything at all without being guided by a belief or set of beliefs, whether it's conscious or unconscious.

You may or may not be able to delineate it, but you have a distinct belief system that has developed over the course of your life. Your earliest beliefs were formed in the context of your family life. Others were born from experiences outside the household. Whatever the basis of your beliefs, they are foundational points of view that you instinctively apply to various areas of your life every day.

Some of your perspectives serve you well. Others do not. Some are based in truth, while some are based on distortions of the truth. For example, if your father was disengaged from your childhood development, you probably made some assumptions about his behavior. You might have assumed that all fathers (or even men in general) are, by definition, aloof. You might have assumed that your father's failure to engage was about you, when it was really about him. You might have inferred that you were unlovable or unworthy of your father's attention—or of anyone else's attention, for that matter. And this belief could have tainted your future relationships.

Regardless of whether your beliefs are based in truth or fiction, they produce corresponding outcomes and impact the writing of your life story.

Motives

Assumptions aren't the only things that are founded on your beliefs. What you believe also becomes your motivation for acting.

Imagine again that you grew up feeling unworthy of a father's attention. Now suppose that you are sixteen years old and navigating the choppy waters of dating. How might your approach to dating be framed by your beliefs? Assuming that you still believe you don't deserve attention, you might unconsciously sabotage your own dating relationships. Expecting *not* to be seen as desirable, you would also expect *not* to be asked out—and you would act accordingly. Or, if you are in a position to ask out someone else, you might expect to be turned down. In either case, you might shy away from such disappointments by avoiding the opposite sex altogether. This, of course, would cement the fulfillment of your expectations.

Alternately, you might take the opposite tack and try too hard to make yourself appealing and available. Believing that you were "created to be ignored," you might be motivated, at an subconscious level, to "beg" for attention, either by dressing provocatively or by clinging to those whose notice you crave.

You can see that when your motives spring from skewed beliefs, your actions and outcomes will reinforce your assumptions.

Metaphors

Metaphors are figures of speech. They express ideas by way of comparison, using one thing to mean another. Take this statement, for example: "My laptop is a dinosaur." The idea is obviously not literal, but the word *dinosaur* indicates the concept of extinction. Anyone who hears the comparison knows almost instinctively what is meant—that the device is so old, it is virtually obsolete.

Do you recall the hypothetical story involving the trip from Portland, Maine, to New York City? That was not a metaphor but an analogy I used to explain the abstract concept of *the gap* in terms of something more concrete (a road trip). Now, imagine that the character in the analogy was a former college football star. Like most people, he uses metaphors extensively in everyday speech. The metaphors he chooses not only explain what he wants to say but also express his feelings and his view of the world.

For metaphors to be useful, their symbolic meaning has to be recognizable. Suppose the former football player used sports metaphors to tell his story. It might sound something like this:

> I thought my hotel was right outside Boston, but it was in Portsmouth. I went to bed thinking I was already at the fifty-yard line, but I was back on my own twenty. When I realized my mistake, I threw a Hail Mary pass. I took every shortcut and blew every speed limit I could. I was third and long, baby, and this interview was *years* in the making. When I walked into that meeting, I put on my game face and headed for the end zone.

Two things need to be said here: Blowing speed limits is a bad idea, and using that many metaphors in an eighty-seven-word account is overkill. Yet most people would experience the story in a more visceral way because the storyteller used metaphors to convey his feelings and perceptions.

Many linguists estimate that the average person uses metaphor more than once in every minute of conversation, not as mere decorative additions to his speech but as information carriers. The very word *metaphor* supports this idea. It comes from the same root as the word *amphora*, which was "an ancient Greek vessel used for carrying and storing precious liquids."[4]

Your metaphors are meaningful, so take stock of those you tend to use. When someone asks how your job is going, do you say, "It's a war zone"? He'll understand the metaphor, but what does it tell you? Does it reveal something you need to know about your thinking? Does it describe the way you interact with others? What information can you glean from your choice of words?

Symbols

Symbols are signs that are widely recognized because of their long-term association with common objects or phenomena. However, because they do not typically resemble what they stand for, we have to learn what they mean. For instance, what comes to mind when you see a red cross? I think you would agree that it signifies the rendering of aid and assistance to those who urgently need it. The cross is not an actual picture of someone rendering or receiving aid, but the symbol has been linked to the concept for so many years that it is universally understood.

Symbols express complex concepts in simple ways. They are often used within metaphors, as we saw in the account I shared from the point of view of a former football player. The *end zone* was symbolic of his goal to ace his interview and get the job. The *Hail Mary pass* was symbolic of his desperate effort to get to New York on time. It illustrated his belief that he had just one chance to land his dream job.

In the parlance of psychology, "symbols are discrete elements embedded within the metaphor"[5] in symbolic form. Take the sentence "My chest is as tight as a rock." Symbolically, it matters whether the rock is sharp and can cut or is hard and can't be broken or porous and can soak up liquid. Attributes and functions of symbolic representations are never random because they carry meaning.[6]

The rock is a symbol embedded within in the metaphor. If a man spoke this statement to his cardiologist, the doctor would take steps to prevent or mitigate a possible heart attack. If the same man spoke the same words to his wife after they received bad news about their child, she would not dial 9-1-1; she would realize that his words described the intensity of his emotional state.

Metaphors and symbols are supported deep in the human psyche by structures of thought and feeling. In his book *Image and Pilgrimage in Christian Culture*, Victor Turner discusses structures called *root paradigms*, which are a "higher-order concept than symbols" and contribute to the development of patterns.[7] Peter Senge, in *The Fifth Discipline*, uses the term *mental models* to describe our "deeply held internal images of how the world works, images that limit us to familiar ways of thinking and acting."[8]

The terms sound technical, and they are. But they are more than linguistic jargon. As we become more consciously aware of these structures, we live less at the mercy of seemingly unknown forces and more in the light of our personal power.

> ## symbol
>
> "Something that stands for or suggests something else by reason of relationship, association, convention, or accidental resemblance; *especially*...a visible sign of something invisible <the lion is a *symbol* of courage>...an object or act representing something in the unconscious mind that has been repressed."[9]

Patterns

Every life is marked by patterns. You might know someone who has gone bankrupt numerous times, experienced multiple divorces, or suffered an unusual number of accidents. You might also know people who succeed in most every endeavor and always seem to be in the right place at the right time. That might even describe you!

Whether the patterns in your life are positive or not, they are never accidental. They are the product of structures. The patterns you experience will not change until your life structures do. These structures might not be self-evident at first. (Typically, they hide in blind spots.) But as you become a more conscious writer of your story, you will uncover the structures that create your patterns.

Just as metaphors carry information, patterns provide deep insights into how our storylines are written. The information revealed is not always welcome. Especially in a self-admiration society, we would rather believe that our negative patterns are random occurrences or someone else's fault. But if we will take ownership of the good *and* bad patterns in our lives, we can live intentionally, and powerfully!

Don't be intimidated by the patterns in your life. Now is the time to yank them out of the closet, tug on their coded threads of information, and acknowledge what they are producing. The benefits of this process are many. Here are just a few:

+ Your patterns will help explain your current reality (the present).

+ Your patterns will reveal how your current reality developed (the past).

+ Your patterns will spark innovations that impact the part of your journey that is ahead (the future).

Past, present, and future clarified simultaneously—that is a coach's dream, so *go for it!* Just let your patterns speak, and be open to what they have to say. For example, you might have a history of being or feeling abandoned, or running from promising opportunities, or avoiding certain situations or particular types of people. When these patterns surface, the experience can be painful, depending upon the depth of the pattern and what it has cost you (quality of life, professional fulfillment, rewarding relationships, etc.). Don't run from the pain. There is great value in processing it!

Your Story Is Bigger than You Think

So what does all of this have to do with navigating the gap? The answer is *everything.* Your life pivots with every gap you navigate, and everyone around you is affected by it.

If you were the special guest on a modern-day version of *This Is Your Life,* the ripple effect of your story would amaze you. People would tell about the intersection of your journey and theirs. They would share the precious moments when you ignited something in their hearts. They would remind you that you are part of something bigger than you think—a community or *tribe* of people whose journeys are intertwined.

Your journey is no ordinary trip. You are about to see that it is *a pilgrimage*.

Sounding the Depths

1. Describe, from your subjective view, the power you have in writing your story. How might an outsider describe it more objectively?

2. How willing are you to fail? How has this helped or hindered your journey?

3. Describe a personal belief that, to the best of your knowledge, is based in truth. Describe another that you now realize is based in deception. What has been the impact of each?

4. Have you uncovered any motives that are based in wrong beliefs? Explain.

5. Have you uncovered any detrimental patterns in your life? Do they control you, or are you empowered to change them? Explain.

Notes

1. See *Merriam-Webster's 11th Collegiate Dictionary*, electronic version, © 2003, s.v. "narrative."
2. "Career Leaders in Striking Out," Baseball Almanac, http://www.baseball-almanac.com/hitting/histrk1.shtml.
3. "Mickey Mantle," Baseball-Reference.com, http://www.baseball-reference.com/players/m/mantlmi01.shtml.
4. Penny Tompkins and James Lawley, "Meta, Milton and Metaphor: Models of Subjective Experience," The Clean Collection (first published in *Rapport*, journal of the Association for NLP [UK], Issue 36, August 1996), http://www.cleanlanguage.co.uk/articles/articles/2/1/Meta-Milton-Metaphor-Models-of-Subjective-Experience/Page1.html.
5. Ibid.
6. Ibid.
7. Victor Turner and Edith Turner, *Image and Pilgrimage in Christian Culture* (New York: Columbia University Press, 1978), 248.
8. Peter M. Senge, *The Fifth Discipline: The Art & Practice of the Learning Organization* (New York: Doubleday, 2006), 163.
9. *Merriam-Webster's 11th Collegiate Dictionary*, electronic version, ©2003, s.v. "symbol."

4

Journey and Pilgrimage

Pilgrimage. For most people, it is a mystical and mysterious word evoking harrowing treks to Tibetan mountain temples, grueling walks over broken glass, or solemn trips to sacred sites.

Pilgrimage is practical and purposeful yet rarely easy. Not always guided by religious beliefs, it is, nevertheless, a journey with spiritual and moral implications. A pilgrimage can be a physical trip to a real place. But it can also be metaphorical. Instead of a physical expedition to hallowed ground, the metaphorical pilgrimage is an inner sojourn in which the pilgrim taps into the recesses of the heart and crosses the unseen threshold between the conscious and unconscious realms.

Thresholds are a defining feature of gap navigation. The threshold between the conscious and the unconscious is the quintessential, invisible seam where the obvious and the hidden brush against each other. As intangible as the place is, no one leaves it unchanged. Even those who refuse to cross the threshold are changed merely by seeing a glimpse of it.

The pilgrim does not resist the threshold and is undeterred by its jagged edges. He or she is no longer willing to be bound by familiar shores, knowing that whatever the journey reveals will be worth more than the price of passage.

The life of intentionality is, by its nature, a pilgrimage. It will wrest you from the place of business as usual and thrust you onto the living edge, where feelings and emotions speak plainly, and needs cannot be addressed with the limited resources of the intellect.

Pilgrimage will cause you to draw from the well of your deepest desires, because they are seminal to a changed way of life. These desires are not wrapped up in self. They reveal whatever wants to happen. They produce no shame and deny no legitimate purpose. They lift you, the sojourner, above programs and predictability, beyond denial and discouragement.

No one starts a pilgrimage until something inside him refuses to tolerate the status quo any longer. The pilgrim embarks on his journey because the confinement of routine and the absence of renewal have become unbearable. He can no longer live within the bounds of what is considered socially polite or tailored for comfort.

To launch into the gap and embrace its riches, pilgrims have to first reach a breaking point in which their feelings and desires *must* be deciphered so the truth *can be* known. They realize the importance of the intellect, but they also know that it is trained to rationalize what is deep and essential while clinging to what no longer belongs. Pilgrims understand that the conscious mind harbors comfortable attachments and prefers to live in chapters that have already ended. It is squeamish about new ones, even those freshly stocked with opportunity.

> Pilgrimage is where the fear of exposing what rages within is set aside for the chance to explore all that is ahead—new and untested, but authentic and alive.

The Sailboat and the "Seam"

An illustration makes the threshold between the conscious and the unconscious plain. Picture a body of water, and then distinguish between its *surface* and *the deep* (the volumes of water below the surface). Now imagine a sailboat afloat on the surface. You can see the boat and the surface it rests upon, but you cannot see much of the deep. You might even ignore what is beneath until dangerous currents demand your attention.

The place of contact shared by the sailboat and the water is a border comparable to the seam between your conscious and unconscious mind. In psychology, this is called the *liminal space*. You will see its workings later; for now, just know that the place exists.

We don't focus on this "seam," because we are not sure where it is or how to find it. It is so uncertain, so unfamiliar, that we withdraw from even the idea of it, as well as from the depths beneath it. In doing so, we forfeit vast opportunities to live consciously and powerfully.

Assuming that you are like most people, you are in denial, to some degree, about the existence of the deep, unexplored waters beneath your surface. The degree of your denial is not as important as your realizing that you don't know what you don't know. Until you arrive at the threshold between the conscious and unconscious realms and agree to explore it, you do not and cannot see how denial and other forms of resistance are working against you.

The threshold, by its nature, sparks crisis. A moment before you arrived at the seam, you lived in blissful yet costly ignorance, unaware of the currents dictating your path. Now you cannot help but see what was hidden. Even if you choose to flee, pretending that looking away is the answer, you will drag with you the albatross of knowing what needs to be addressed.

Owning a conscious awareness of your inner reality is the only wise choice. If you avoid dealing with the resistances that were hidden till now, you will continue to block your route to transformation. You might continue bobbing on the surface of your life, but that sea will ride you—and hard.

True transformation above the seam is not possible. It must occur beneath, where unresolved emotions, misperceptions, and feelings of rejection, self-negation, and the like operate. Dealing with these deep issues is the only way to be free.

Until you understand what is feeding your turmoil, you will project onto your experiences *whatever it is you think life has "done" to you*. Then, having assigned blame, you will file your issues away in your "Case Closed" folder, as though the matter were resolved. You will feel relieved and empowered to say, "I won't do this anymore"—i.e., "I won't erupt in any more fits of rage. I won't placate others in exchange for their approval. I won't bury my pain under emotional eating or any other form of self-medication."

As sincere as you may be, you will find yourself repeating the unwanted behavior, probably within three days' time. Why? Because no transformation has occurred. The same resistances are still in place. All you did was give them new labels and new places to hide.

Remember who is writing your narrative—*you*. And you're writing it using metaphors and symbols that speak to your senses and float on the border between the conscious and the unconscious. Let your metaphors speak to you, as they do to others. Allow them to expose the contents of the deep waters. Then, be willing to penetrate the seam so that the story you are writing is no longer a mystery to you.

Desire Liberated

The word *desire* is charged with emotion, so let's frame it in the context of pilgrimage. Remember that desire is seminal to the journey. Although food, sex, and other pleasures are important to life and serve larger purposes, this conversation is not about desire in those terms. It is about the thirst for something that reaches beyond self and self-gratification.

For example, we thirst for physical and emotional wholeness, for fulfilling relationships, for places to invest our talents and treasures so that they may produce fruit and profit others. Acknowledging and prioritizing our desires is especially important when meaning is lacking, even to the point where an existential vacuum exists. This is where unquenched desires scream the loudest—and where we most want to ignore them.

When meaning is missing, we reach for substitutes and try to satisfy our desires in unhealthy ways. We attempt to numb our pain with "fixes" that are as superficial and fleeting as the relief they provide. In the end, our pain increases, and the existential hole deepens.

Substitutes simply cannot satisfy. Ignatius Loyola, the founder of the Jesuit order of Roman Catholicism, understood this truth. As a young man in the fifteenth century, he was inspired by "ideals of courtly love and knighthood."[1] After he sustained severe wounds in battle, his desire to achieve was unabated, but his planned course was rearranged. Instead of becoming a knight, he became a follower of Christ. His conversion released in him new desires that helped him to clarify his ultimate purpose and path. What used to belong on his path—dreams of chivalry in battle—was moved aside, so that what really belonged—a passion for spiritual pursuits—could take its place.

Ignatius described seven attitudes essential to discerning one's purpose. He wrote in the context of the divine will, but his thoughts are meaningful, whatever your worldview. One item in his studies involves knowing the difference between *ends* and *means*. Ignatius observed that people tend to confuse the two and attempt to satisfy their legitimate needs with unfulfilling substitutes.

He explained his point by describing poor choices. In one example, he wrote about people who marry not with serving in mind but with marriage as a goal unto itself. Ignatius saw marriage differently—not as an end in itself but as a means of serving God and others by honoring the institution He created.

Ignatius also discussed money and the poor financial decisions people often make:

> Many people first choose to make a lot of money or to be successful, and only afterwards to be able to serve God by it....In other words, they mix up the order of an end and a means to that end. What they ought to seek first and above all else, they often put last.[2]

Do you see how easily we can turn desire inside out? Ignatius sought to liberate desire from false motives so that it could move us toward well-being. He knew that confusing ends with means would lead to a darkened understanding of how life was designed to work. We would end up marrying for money, sacrificing family for career, and satisfying our base appetites instead of seeking out our higher callings. Until we have clarity in this area, we will squander our integrity and heap dissatisfaction upon ourselves.

Have your means and ends become tangled in a headlong search for fulfillment? Can you pinpoint some examples? Is this the first time you became consciously aware of the switch?

Pilgrimage and History

For centuries, people have made pilgrimages to special places where miracles occurred in the past, are occurring in the present, or are expected to occur in the future. The Celts called them the *thin places* "where two worlds meet."[3] In a metaphorical pilgrimage, it is the *liminal space* I mentioned earlier—a transformative gap and the definitive teachable space.

This was not an everyday place. In ancient and even medieval times, for the most part, the ordinary person was born, lived, and died in the same village. Economic, vocational, and relational aspects of life played out within the same atmospheres and geographic spaces, with a limited cast of characters.

With routines so rigid, times of personal renewal were hard to find. There was one exception: the religious pilgrimage. A small subset of common folk was fortunate enough to break free, however rarely, from the demands of survival in order to taste *the* great luminal experience in the life of faith.

For most people, pilgrimage was the only respite from the unyielding structures of life. This is not to say that spiritual pilgrimages were made only to escape the mundane. Sojourners understood that escape from the habitual was an important part of the renewal process. They also understood that pilgrimage was much more than fun and games.

Pilgrims faced a host of dangers and uncertainties along the way. Exposure to the elements and threats of attack by wild beasts or bands of thieves and robbers were common. Death was a real possibility. Yet pilgrims weighed these risks against the journey's reward. They longed to break out of one world—the world of everyday survival—in order to explore the world of transformation, renewal, and the miraculous.

One famous ancient pilgrimage lasted forty years and transformed two nations. This was the exodus of the Israelites from slavery in Egypt to freedom in the Promised Land. (See the book of Exodus.) The risks were great and, to the Israelites alive at that time, unknown. As a people, they were unaccustomed to travel and had grown used to being provided for by their masters. The exodus would demand a total paradigm shift. Not only would they leave their predictable routines behind, but they would also journey through harsh wilderness environments. Even basic provision for a group their size was entirely beyond their means.

Pilgrimage is not for the faint of heart. It is for those whose desire overcomes their fear. Pilgrimage has a purpose, and transformation and new levels of freedom are its rewards.

The Purpose and Rewards of Pilgrimage

Today, many millions of pilgrims are far more mobile and far less confined to their homes. For the most part, they also face far fewer dangers as they travel hundreds and even thousands of miles to the Holy Land, Mecca, Lourdes, Rome, and so forth.

Yet, the dynamics of the pilgrimage have changed very little. When pilgrims travel today, they still have a destination in mind. They know they cannot reach it without leaving business as usual behind. Although they rarely fear dying of thirst or starving to death in the desert, they know they must lay some part of themselves and their fortunes on the line if they are to explore the thin places. And they know there is no reward without risk.

Pilgrims are intentional about the risks and rewards of the journey. They expect to incur both. The same is true of those on a metaphorical pilgrimage. Their risks and rewards are discovered as they cross the line between the unconscious and the conscious mind. Once there, they must identify and discard any old baggage that would hinder them on the journey. They must locate and set aright any internal structures that have kept them locked up in old places. And to make the pilgrimage profitable, they must tap into and activate the power to live intentionally and to own their stories.

The gains to be made are potentially huge, for pilgrimage leads to...

Release from Internal Hindrances

This is the pilgrim's "get out of jail card," but it is not exactly free. When you break with business as usual, you discover what has been imprisoning you. Once it is uncovered, the structures that contradict your purpose can be dismantled—but only if you are willing to live without them!

Imagine for a moment that you uncover structures of self-pity and a victim mentality stemming from childhood experiences with emotional abuse. Your grievances are real and terrible. *You were an innocent victim who deserved much better.* But your current relationships are made toxic by your unconscious desire to be pitied *now*. In a misguided and ultimately futile attempt to get your due, you use your "victim card" with people who have not abused you and who cannot repay the debt of your abusers.

Pilgrimage has led you to the threshold between the conscious and the unconscious mind. You stand face-to-face with the swirling feelings you have never been able to quite pinpoint. You've known all along that you are hurting and that your relationships are failing, but now you know why and where it all began. You are not done, however. Healing is under way, but it will not be evident until you:

1. Forgive your abusers. This does not mean excusing their actions but rather releasing them from an enormous debt that they can never repay.

2. Sacrifice the fleeting satisfaction derived from self-pity and from playing the victim, so that you can live powerfully and joyfully, while assuming appropriate responsibility for your outcomes.

Unless you *allow* pilgrimage to release you from your internal hindrances, you will carry the albatross of knowing what is wrong while refusing to address it.

Integration Within That Produces All-around Wholeness

When we are imprisoned by internal structures operating in the unconscious mind, we become fragmented. Competing states of consciousness and unconsciousness produce misunderstanding, self-sabotage, and an uneven journey of fits and starts. Brokenness leaves us aware that something is missing or out of place, yet we remain unsure of *what* is broken or *where* the fragments should be. The dysfunction leaves us vulnerable to increasing fragmentation as we endeavor to build new structures to mask or manage our pain.

The pilgrimage from the unconscious realm to the conscious begins the transformation process by first revealing the structures that mark our disintegration. We can then elect to demolish them and make way for healthy new structures that promote integration and support wholeness.

Only those who are willing to *complete* this journey know the wholeness that pilgrimage can yield.

Liberation from Social Structures That Hinder Genuine Freedom

The Israelites served as slaves in Egypt for more than four hundred years. They did not go to Egypt with slavery in mind. At first, they were welcomed and protected by Pharaoh. But when the political climate changed, their status changed along with it. New leaders established social structures that stripped the Hebrews of the favor they once enjoyed. The exodus, with all its challenges, was designed to liberate the Israelites from the political, physical, social, and psychological effects of enslavement, and to prepare them to rule their own land.

Of course, you can be entrapped in a hindering social structure without becoming a literal slave. But what if you feel like a captive of your environment? Do you live in a neighborhood marked by gang culture? Gang activity is a social hindrance, and an overtly dangerous one, at that. Yet you do not forfeit all hope of success in life just because gangs trouble your neighborhood and your life. There are antidotes to this negative structure. Having a solid family life, getting a good education, and articulating goals and dreams that rise above the surrounding culture are part of that pathway.

Whether you choose to relocate or to stay and become part of the solution, you must face what is. Your pilgrimage can be as simple as awakening to the social structures that seem to hem you in. Once awakened, you will face decisions that cover more than your physical location. They may be more about how you choose to live, *wherever* you live.

Your decisions are the key. The word *decide* comes from the Latin *decidere*, which means "to cut off."[4] When faced with multiple paths, you can choose only one; you must "cut off" all possible alternatives. In the above example, whether you decide that you need to relocate and further your education or stay put and help the surrounding community, you must "cut off" any structure that would distract from your decision or contradict your purpose.

A Discovery of the Truthfulness of the Tribe

You do not live out your life or fulfill your destiny in isolation. Your tribe is a social container that shares a consensus that existed before you arrived and will continue to exist long after you depart. That shared belief system is a structure. It includes the belief that you, and all members of your community, have a unique potential to develop and contribute to the betterment of the tribe. Knowing this is important to achieving your outcomes, because it affirms that your life has meaning, and it refutes the existential vacuum.

Theologian Walter Brueggemann refers to "the trustful truth of the tribe."[5] It is proof that you are not isolated but needed. That is not to say that the tribe determines your place or position. Those must be discovered by you. No one else can determine or assign your destiny. But trusted people can mirror back their experiences to you. Their lives might be very different from yours, but their insights often contain universal truths that correspond with your journey and will shed light on it.

This is why we read the biographies of people we have never met. Their narratives provide clues about intentional living, and they help us to identify the unique seasons, cycles, and gaps we are experiencing. Yet, their lives are not meant to become templates for us to follow. In a culture geared toward conformity, it is all too easy to adopt someone else's path or even to co-opt the direction of the community. The cultural pull of the tribe is strong, and we have been conditioned to conform to the pack.

The "trustful truth of the tribe" is important. The guidance of those who went before you is valuable; and yet, unconscious surrender to anything that contradicts your larger purpose is counterproductive. There are longstanding truths in every tribe. Some of them inform your path; some reveal what does not belong. Allow the trustful truth of the tribe to release your creativity, inspire innovation, and provoke original thought.

Suppose you were born in a culture that forbade leadership by women. Now imagine that your family immigrated to the United States, where you were hired by a large corporation. How will you react when your immediate supervisor—a woman—corrects your work or offers tips for your success? Will you accept her coaching graciously, or will your belief system prevent you from growing under her leadership?

The Dynamics and Perils of Pilgrimage

Whatever the cost of pilgrimage, it is your opportunity to follow your desire into a new, fertile space. Has this kind of yearning tugged at your heart? Does it arrest you at unexpected moments and cause you to question particular patterns in your life? Have you wondered aloud, "Will this *ever* change?"

If so, you can be sure something is percolating beneath the surface of your life and begging for your attention. Do not run from it or stifle the tug for fear of upsetting your status quo. Respond to the tug by *leveraging it*. An inner pilgrimage may be calling. It will cost you something, but it just might blaze a path to the life you once thought impossible.

To leverage the call, you must understand what it entails. Although you probably won't travel through difficult terrain, adverse climate conditions, criminal elements, or the epidemics faced by pilgrims in past centuries, you can learn from the perils they faced and consider how they might apply to your life. Here is a short list of hardships they faced that may sound familiar as you travel forward:

+ *Trials to test fidelity, integrity, virtue, and constancy.* Pilgrimage offered a welcome change but also produced new stresses and opportunities to stumble. Failure was a real possibility, and the cost of failure could be great.

In metaphorical pilgrimage, the greatest risk is to the status quo, but the unfamiliarity of the gap can leave you feeling less surefooted and confident of what is next and of who you are. To muster a sense of security, however false, you might be tempted to cut corners to ensure against embarrassment. Resist the temptation. Be true to yourself, and allow the journey to uproot your fears.

+ *Tribulations, specifically the pressures experienced in the narrow places of pilgrimage.* A simple camping trip proves how quickly your options can disappear. Freshwater sources are questionable. Cooking is more difficult. Support systems are left behind. Imagine the contingencies during pilgrimage! Those who make the physical trek must function with less, and master their limitations.

The same is true of metaphorical pilgrimage. It will take you through narrow places where experience does not serve, where your customary "go-to" responses fail to produce the desired results. The breaking of stifling paradigms always produces surges in pressure—especially the pressure to retreat or to disqualify yourself from the journey.

• *Temptations that could cause the pilgrim to lapse into sin or out of faith.* Remember that travel was entirely foreign to people who never expected to venture out from the village. The home environment that stifled them also served to keep them accountable. Once removed from their support system, some pilgrims would indulge secret desires and new "freedoms." Difficulties on the journey could also produce consuming crises of faith.

For the metaphorical pilgrim, the dismantling of familiar structures introduces new lines of thought. Some are positive, but others are not. This is where Ignatius Loyola's ideas about prioritizing and distinguishing *means* from *ends* can be most helpful.

Taking Consciousness Forward

Pilgrimage produces an environment in which dysfunction can be exposed and abandoned, and adventures in radical newness can be enjoyed. The rewards—the miracles of transformation that occur in the thin places—make the journey irresistible!

Forgive me for stating the obvious: Crossing the threshold between the conscious and unconscious realms requires a firm decision, as well as commitment to engage in the process. Only *you* can choose whether and when to take the proverbial plunge. And, as was true for "liminal" pilgrims of old, the routine obligations embedded in your present social structure will be reordered by the new priorities of your pilgrimage. In some ways, you will experience far more freedom as you journey. Choices that seemed impossible "inside the box" become viable when you step outside it. At the same time, the requirements of your journey will limit other choices you once made freely.

Pilgrimage is a journey to progressively deeper levels of awakening. Unless you are intentional and willing to cross your conventional boundaries, your more familiar instincts will betray you. Instead of embracing your destination, you will cling to the way you think your world should be.

So, consider this chapter a challenge from the coach in your pocket: The pilgrim within you is ready to travel.

Sounding the Depths

1. Are you on a pilgrimage, or do you view your life as one? Explain.

2. What is stuffed inside your "Case Closed" folder? What frustrations have resulted? How do you plan to address the real issues behind them?

3. In this chapter, I argued the following: "Pilgrims are intentional about the risks and rewards of the journey. They expect to incur both." How does this statement apply to you? How does it describe the person you are becoming?

4. What evidence of wholeness do you see in your life? Where is fragmentation revealed? What, in your opinion, has caused these opposite outcomes, and why?

5. Name three areas in which you need to *decide*—i.e., to "cut off" your alternate route options. How does this clarify your path?

Notes

1. "St. Ignatius Loyola," IgnationSpirituality.com, http://www.ignatianspirituality.com/ignatian-voices/st-ignatius-loyola/.
2. St. Ignatius Loyola, *Spiritual Exercises*, quoted in Warren Sazama, S.J., "Some Ignatian Principles for Making Prayerful Decisions," Marquette.edu/Faith, http://www.marquette.edu/faith/ignatian-principles-for-making-decisions.php.
3. Turner and Turner, *Image and Pilgrimage in Christian Culture*, xli.
4. *Merriam-Webster's 11th Collegiate Dictionary*, electronic version, © 2003, s.v. "decide."
5. Walter Brueggemann, *David's Truth in Israel's Imagination and History, Second Edition* (Minneapolis, MN: Augsburg Fortress, 2002).

5

The Inadvertent Designer

Whether you are an iconic figure with a global reputation or someone known only by a small circle of people, you are a world-class designer. You have been designing all your life, even when you had no idea that you could. What have you designed, you ask? The answer is, *your life.*

It's true! The sum total of your life, to this point, has been custom crafted by you, and your masterpiece is making an impact. Does that sound like an overstatement? It isn't. Just consider the ramifications of a single life (in this case, *your* life). You affect many people, even when you think you are going it alone. The effect you have is formed and revealed at the level of certain structures in your life, including environment, beliefs, identity, and others.

Your perceptions also play an enormous role in your design, so much so that your life takes the shape of them. Before you had the slightest clue about structures and journeys—before you were consciously aware of symbols and narratives or the fact that you even had a story—you were sculpting a narrative from your experiences and your interpretations of them.

Whether your story has materialized as you once dared to hope, or whether it has exceeded your wildest dreams, it is *yours.* Of course, I don't know anyone who wouldn't like a second crack at the drawing board. Even those who have lived with practiced intentionality have gotten less-than-perfect results from time to time.

But what if your role as life designer is coming as a complete surprise at this very moment? What if you are just now realizing that you started your journey without any intentions of any kind? What if you are the quintessentially inadvertent designer?

The truth is that all of us have inadvertently designed certain aspects of our lives. But here's another truth: As long as we are breathing, there is more designing yet to do.

Responding to Inadvertent Structures

Few people realize how involved they have been and are in the development of their own stories. Instead of working with mental blueprints to build their lives, brick by thoughtful brick, they see themselves as outsiders looking in on the building process. They live from day to day, year to year, decade to decade, unaware that bricks are slipping into place with precious little intent or conscious guidance.

That is a lousy way to build a life, and an even more unsatisfying way to live. Instead of building with purpose and enjoying the fruits of their labor, serially inadvertent designers spend much of their energy stumbling from one debris pile to another, wondering all the while who let the construction site get out of hand.

Sadly, their plight is a common one. It is a lifestyle of trial and error, and one that brings on unnecessary turmoil. It produces rolling waves of seismic activity in the inner life, along with clawing chaos and instability that create cracks in surface structures.

Remember that everything in your life has a structure. Your current reality has a structure. When it becomes flawed, you experience dissatisfaction. If you are aware and intentional, this symptom will lead you to inspect the structure for clues. You might find a "crack" or some other flaw in the "foundation." Whatever you find, the discovery is good news, because your "building" can be fixed!

Nevertheless, there are two prerequisites to improving your life design: You have to desire a change in your current reality, and you have to cooperate with the "remodel." Your desired reality cannot emerge without your permission and participation. There is effort involved, because improvements don't happen by your wishing for them. They happen as you cooperate with the inner work that produces outer change.

Inside and out, your life is a structure of levels, as you'll soon see. And they are interconnected, so that a change to one affects all the others. The foundation impacts the levels above it, but those levels also affect the foundation. Be prepared for this to happen, because the change you desire will cause all the structures in your life to shift. This should not be viewed as unwelcome collateral damage but a welcome realignment that produces wholeness.

Welcome to Your House

You are the general contractor in charge of building your life—your "house." Whether you are eighteen or eighty-eight, your house remains a work in progress. You live in it, not by compulsion but by choice. After all, you built it!

This concept is absolutely necessary to grasp. You are *not* a marionette on the string of an unseen force who decides what your life should look like. You are a human being with the power to see, think, feel, decide, and act. You are always thinking something. Your thoughts flow continuously, whether you consciously heed them or not. Because you are always thinking, you are always deciding and acting. This is true, even when you decide *not* to decide or to act at all!

Do you see how we become inadvertent designers of the structure called life? Even when we try to "play it safe" by opting out of the process, we are building something. In fact, *not acting* is the most foolproof way to build badly. We do it from a thought process—a structure—that says, "I have no power to act in this situation. It is already out of my control. I'll just sit this one out and let it blow over."

Please read this statement several times, to let it sink in: *The perception of powerlessness has no basis in reality.* To be human is to have inherent power to think, decide, and act. If you have no power, then you must not be a human being. If you insist that you are human (and you are), you must also insist that, even when you *feel* powerless, you still *have* power.

The perception of powerlessness is a perversion of truth. Yet even perversions of truth can build things. The trouble is that they build the very things we wish to avoid, and they prove an unpleasant reality: *If we fail to use our inherent power, we forfeit the rightful authority we have been given over our own lives.*

An important caveat must be restated here: No human being who is operating in natural human capacities has ultimate control over nature or other people. If your best friend insists on surfing the waves of a tsunami, your attempts to either stop the wave or supersede your friend's free will as a human being will produce disappointing results for both of you. You will be frustrated in trying to help someone who refuses to be helped; he or she will be frustrated to learn that tsunamis do not take orders from concerned friends.

To renovate your "inadvertently designed house," you must own your personal power and become purposeful about making changes. The transformation you desire begins when you honor the power that has been entrusted to you. Again, no one has more power over your life than you do. No one else is responsible (or can be responsible) for what you think, say, do, and feel. As too many of us have learned the hard way, no one gets a pass on this fact—not even those who were treated unfairly or whose upbringings were deficient in some way. As unfair and unpleasant as life can be, we remain free to choose what comes next. Life can get better, or it can get worse. It is our call.

Does this line of reasoning speak to you? Are you seeing areas of your life that could be handled differently? The choices you have made, and are making at this moment, determine the ongoing design of your house. None of it is set in stone, however. It's your house, and you can renovate it any time you choose. If you want to add a front porch, build one. If you prefer an open design, go for it. Whatever you want your house to look like, *just build it.*

Our outcomes are directly tied to our use of the power we have been given. In our society of self-admiration, we find it easier to blame others than to accept responsibility. By shifting blame, we relinquish the power we have, and thereby create potentially endless cycles of powerlessness. There is a better choice—the choice to exercise dominion over the one thing nobody else can rule. And that is *ourselves*.

Belief Goes to Work

Phenomenal possibilities are lying dormant in every life, including yours. If they remain dormant, the possibilities become moot. No benefit or pleasure will be gained from them, regardless of how phenomenal they may be. The possibility that you *could* earn a seven-figure income won't pay the bills, as they say.

You can revive the possibilities inherent within you by acknowledging them, appropriating them, and consciously applying yourself to their fulfillment. You do this (or choose not to do it) according to what you believe. Even your unspoken beliefs are more potent than you probably realize. If you believe that your talent is great but that no one is interested in what you can do, you *will* find a way, at an unconscious level, to ensure that no one is interested in what you can do. If, on the other hand, if you believe that you can make a difference, regardless of the obstacles, you *will* make a difference, regardless of the obstacles.

The story of NFL running back Derrick Coleman is an outstanding example of how our beliefs go to work.[1] As a child, he was diagnosed with an incurable hearing loss that left him legally deaf. The disability created a host of challenges. Kids berated and bullied Coleman in the schoolyard. Learning was more complicated for him than for most other children. And learning to speak was especially difficult.

Coleman's hearing problem also threatened something bigger and even more important to him: his dream to play football. Players must be able to hear the quarterback, a task that is hard enough for those whose hearing is not impaired, due to the crowd noise in NFL stadiums. Although

Coleman wore hearing aids, they didn't solve his problem. Instead, they produced noisy feedback and distracted him more than they helped.

Coleman was told, over and over again, that someone with his condition could never make the cut in the NFL. Yet Coleman never stopped trying. He excelled in high school football and advanced to UCLA. At some point, his mother solved the hearing-aid feedback problem by cutting up several pairs of pantyhose and using the stretchy strips to hold her son's hearing aids in place. Pursuing his dream had become a family affair, and everyone played a part in keeping it alive.

Derrick Coleman became the first deaf man in NFL history to play offense.[2] Achieving his dream was not easy. It required a lifetime of "adjustments on the playing field."[3] It forced him to work harder than everyone else. He had to prove his ability to compete with the best hearing players in the world. And he proved it because he *believed* he could do it. He accepted the reality of his deafness and owned his power to overcome the challenges it caused him.

Coleman also accepted accountability for his disadvantage. He said, "When [coaches] put someone on the field, they don't want to have no doubt in their mind....[You have to] get the job done regardless."[4]

That's ownership! Derrick Coleman built the structure of his life on the facts of his talent and on the belief that a deaf man could make it in the NFL. On February 2, 2014, he followed his belief all the way to the Super Bowl, and his team, the Seattle Seahawks, won big!

Structure and Your Current Reality

Your current reality is an outward manifestation of something inward. Deeper structures of belief and ownership produced fulfillment in the outward reality of Derrick Coleman's professional life. But how many hearing-impaired players were driven off by their beliefs? How many said, "I would play football if I could, but I can't, because my hearing is impaired"?

The rationalization is understandable, but the cost is high.

Coleman pushed past his obvious predicament and took ownership of the inner structures of his life. Because he did, he was free to advance confidently in the direction of his future, regardless of his disability. Throughout his life, he built layers of structure within his heart and mind by which he faced potential barriers with a conscious and purposeful intentionality, rendering them inconsequential.

The structure of Coleman's life determined his outcome. And the structure of your life will do the same. Either it will draw lines of limitation around your life, keeping you locked in cycles and patterns of the past, or it will release you into your potential and destiny.

The choice is yours. First, you must recognize the structures that are in play. Second, you must understand their connection to your current reality. This means taking a look at the surface structures as well as the layers of deeper or hidden structures.

You don't have to be a psychology major to do this. Just keep reading!

Deep Structures Versus Surface Structures

Robert Dilts, a key voice in the field of neuro-linguistic programming (NLP), has developed critical insights into the structures we have been discussing. An overview of his ideas about deep structures and surface structures will shed light on our coaching conversation.

> Tangible behaviors, expressions, and reactions are "surface structures" which are the result of bringing "deeper structures" into reality....It is frequently important to examine multiple examples of surface structures in order to better know or identify the deeper structure which produces it. Another way to think about the relationship between deep structure and surface structure is the distinction between "process" and "product." Products are the surface level expressions of the deeper and less tangible generative processes which are their source.[5]

In other words, things that can be seen—your behaviors, expressions, and reactions—are surface structures generated by the deeper, less visible structures you have designed. This concept has a lot to do with your inherent creativity. You are creative, even if you don't think you are. In fact, you are always creating something. The question is whether you are using your creativity to your best advantage. In other words, is your creativity taking you closer to the fulfillment of your purpose or further away from it, and why?

What you create depends on what you perceive. Your perceptions of how the world works will channel your creative juices in one direction or another. So, what do your *perceptions* inspire? Do they lead to sound *conceptions* of your life and world? Do they produce goal-affirming actions that support your stated intentions, or are they contradicting your purpose and fighting your dream at every turn?

If you aspire to play in the NFL, for example, are your perceptions of your natural abilities accurate? Have they inspired a sound plan of action in keeping with your goals? Are you committed to a fitness regimen and to living a healthy lifestyle? Are you developing your skill set or just maintaining it? Are your goals and habits aligned with the expectations and culture of the NFL?

Your answers to these questions will be tied to the way your life is structured and to the level of your awareness of that structure. If you have been designing your life unconsciously, your layers of structure are already working against you. This is why it is so important to recognize your creative role. You have spent the totality of your journey designing your life. If you are surprised by your outcomes, you really shouldn't be, for they are product of your design and bear witness to the choices you have made.

But don't despair. Just take your creativity and start redesigning.

Put Perception and Conception to Work

Like all humans, you are a meaning-maker. You perceive and interpret the signs, symbols, and metaphors that show up in your environment, and your interpretations are directly linked to your habits of perception, which are based largely on your point of view. For example, are you a "glass half full" type, or do you focus on the empty half? Either way, your habits of perception will shape your secondary experiences.

Here is what I mean: Suppose that you are prone to pessimism, and the first love of your life breaks your heart. How do you interpret the event, and how will it affect your future relationships?

Unless you consciously assess the breakup and its impact on your inner landscape, your next relationship could suffer. Why? Because your perception, or interpretation, of that first experience will lead to more general conceptions about love and will correspondingly shape your surface structures (behaviors, expressions, and reactions) as they relate to romantic relationships.

How you react to your experiences always impacts your future outcomes. If you develop such habitual perceptions as "Members of the opposite sex always love me, then leave me," or "He/she must have left me because I am 'less than' other women/men," or "I'm no good at dating," your first relationship debacle probably won't be your last. Instead of seeing your first breakup as a normal part of life, you will view it with shame.

If, however, you take the experience in stride and glean valuable information from it about the kind of relationship you deserve and desire, you will help to build deep structures that are sound, sturdy, and able to support healthy relationships in the future. You will be better positioned to work through relational difficulties and less apt to fall apart when a relationship ends.

> Which of your life experiences, if any, parallel the example of the broken romance I just discussed? What long-term effects did your experience produce?

Your Structures on Paper

Understanding the basic structures undergirding your life can help you to see your emotional and cognitive experiences more clearly. Robert Dilts's work in the area of structure is based, in part, on what famed anthropologist Gregory Bateson called *logical levels*. Dilts "mapped" his own "neuro-logical levels" of the human brain—levels that process our unique ways of thinking and being.[6]

The pyramid below shows Dilts's arrangement, beginning with *environment* at the base and working upward through the topmost level, which is *spirituality/connectedness*. This apex is the level at which your vision becomes reality.

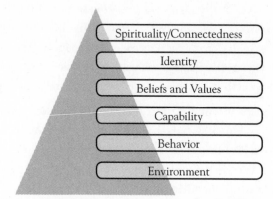

Robert Dilts's Neuro-logical Levels of the Brain[7]

(Reproduced with permission of the author.
Copyright © 1998 by Robert Dilts, Santa Cruz, CA)

Remember that everything has a structure, and that every structure is arranged in a specific ways, whether that structure is a corporation, a family, or a Girl Scout troop. The levels are interrelated, so that each level affects all the levels around it. For our purposes, let's look at the first five levels of Dilts's pyramid, which shows the structures we interact with the most, according to his research.

Environment

Your environment includes your community; your household; your family members, friends, neighbors, and other people who live and work around you; and the structures operating in your environment. Some environments are more challenging than others. All of them contain possibilities and opportunities, but deterrents to those possibilities and opportunities also exist.

You interact with your environment continuously. You find it comfortable or challenging, hot or cold, inviting or forbidding. Your environment causes you to either expand or contract. In the first case, you feel empowered within your environment to breathe deeply and express your life vision. In the second, you feel constrained and less able to express yourself.

Even more important than your environment is your response to it. From a coaching perspective, any aspect of your external environment that is not helpful in creating your desired future warrants examination. Here is why: A closer look will help you to uncover internal issues that need your attention and might otherwise have gone undetected. Chronic distractions are a good example. Find out why they are there and why you tolerate them. Ask yourself what role you play in their presence and what roles they play in your future.

Whether he would explain it in these terms or not, Derrick Coleman did just this. His environment served up persistent distractions that opposed his dream, from the kids who bullied him to the mantra that deaf people can't play football. But instead of tolerating the distractions, he formed an internal environment that allowed him to bypass them.

This was not the easiest route Coleman could have taken. When your environment opposes your vision, the easiest option is to shift blame by finding fault with the environment and resigning yourself to the belief that changing it is an impossible task. This perception leads to a dangerous conception: *I am doomed to failure; therefore, I must relinquish my vision and accept its demise.* When it is internalized and acted on, this deceptive structure becomes a self-fulfilling prophecy.

Here is the rock-solid truth: Your circumstances do not make you or break you; they only reveal you. Whatever is occurring in your environment right now is a surface structure. You might label it as the source of your troubles, but that label comes from a deeper place in your thinking. The only way to expose the deeper structure is to question it. Unless you do, it will keep informing your choices and nourishing future failures.

Don't buy into the fairy tale of ideal environments. The "perfect place" would be chock-full of positive reinforcement coming from every direction at all times. But there is no such environment, and most people do not understand how to reshape their own internal environment. Like most everyone else, they cave to the powers of negative reinforcement.

The truth is that everyone is doing his best to "get by." If you understand this plight, you can avoid becoming entangled in it. No matter what your environment looks like, "getting by" is not your only option. Vision *never* becomes reality by your "just getting by." Vision becomes reality when you become conscious of the features of your environment so that you can use them to maximize your internal landscape.

If you are searching for the perfect environment, you are wasting your time. Do your best to perfect the environment you are already in. Tend to it as though it was your garden of Eden, trusting that all the resources you need to beautify your life are already growing in its soil.

Behavior

Behavior includes your habits, your common actions or activities, and your lifestyle. Behavior is the way you function in your environment, and it reveals how you view that environment. For example, you base your beliefs about your environment on your experiences there. Those experiences, and your responses to them, create your sense of what is real or true. So, if you were raised in an inner-city environment in which gangs seemed to be all-powerful, you might gravitate toward gang membership because you believe it will make *you* powerful.

Such perceptions develop over time as the features of your environment pass through your internal filters. Therefore, if your parents provided a strong system of support and instilled within you values that ascribed strength to superior sources, your internal filter would be more likely to reject gang membership. You might instead seek empowerment in a good education, leading to a meaningful and productive career.

This process, subjective and often unconscious, can easily be distorted by projection. In other words, we tend to see things not as they are but as *we* are. Then, we act on the basis of what we believe, which results in our producing even more of what we are! This is the nature of self-fulfilling prophecies.

Sociologist Robert K. Merton explained it this way:

> The self-fulfilling prophecy is, in the beginning, a *false* definition of the situation evoking a new behavior, which makes the originally false conception come *true*. The specious validity of the self-fulfilling prophecy perpetuates a reign of error. For the prophet will cite the actual course of events as proof that he was right from the very beginning.[8]

Whatever the behavior, it begins with perceptions and ends with those perceptions being confirmed. Another sociologist, W. I. Thomas, made this famous statement: "If men define situations as real, they are real in their consequences."[9] According to Thomas, people react to situations, to the way they perceive situations, and to the meaning they assign to their perceptions.

No wonder we become tangled around the axle in certain areas and situations. We are so invested in our projections that we inadvertently perpetuate the very things we long to eliminate!

Capabilities

Your behaviors are structured largely by your capabilities (including your skills and competencies). If you discover that you have musical talent, for example, you are more likely to take up the violin. And if you become a skilled violinist, you will spend more of your time practicing and performing (i.e., behaving like a violinist). In this example, your behavior springs from an understanding of your capabilities.

But the opposite can also occur: Your behavior can be shaped by a misunderstanding of your capabilities. Do you remember the *mental models* mentioned in chapter 3? Peter Senge used the term to describe "deeply held internal images of how the world works, images that limit us to familiar ways of thinking and acting."[10] Our mental models define many things, including what we *believe* we are capable or incapable of doing.

Even when we are unaware of them, mental models help us form strategies for living. For example, Derrick Coleman firmly believed in his capabilities as a football player, even though he had a reasonable distrust of his hearing. At some level, he believed the world worked in ways that would allow him to progress to the NFL, so he worked the system by striving to play successfully at the high school and collegiate levels. It may have been his confident belief that his hearing problem could be reconciled with the demands of the game, or that his place in the world was that of an NFL running back—or both. In any case, his mental model said, "I can do this."

Deeply held mental models are the lenses through which we see our lives. They serve either to empower or to blind us, to expand our vision or to create blind spots. When our vision is obstructed—especially when we are blind to our own blindness—our perceptions become flawed. Even the greatest violinist can believe that he or she is not skilled enough to play with musicians who, objectively speaking, are far less skilled.

Beliefs and Values

In chapter 3, we talked about beliefs as an element of your story. Beliefs are also important within the context of structures, as they are the guiding force behind your actions and decisions. The more deeply entrenched your beliefs are, the more powerfully they will govern your actions and decisions, and the more they will affect your sense of personal capability.

Beliefs and values work together. If you believe that stealing is wrong, your belief is value-based, and you probably won't pursue a career in bank robbery. Your belief (and maybe your fear of imprisonment) would discourage a life of crime. But how firm is your belief about stealing? How settled are your values? Do they keep you from fudging your tax returns or "borrowing" office supplies from your workplace without the intention of returning them?

The more deeply held your beliefs are, the more organized, layered, and structured they are. They do not magically appear in your mind; they are built, layer by layer, upon the observations and experiences filed in your mental library. Your beliefs and values inform your reasoning and lead to subsequent thoughts, judgments, evaluations, and feelings—all of which affect your decisions and consequent actions. For example, if you were to cheat on your taxes, and the IRS prosecuted you, the unpleasantness of the experience would likely cause you to reconsider repeating such behavior in the future.

You have already seen how beliefs can become self-fulfilling prophecies. But beliefs are powerful in every facet of your thought-life. Just as your environment fosters either expansion or constraint, so do your beliefs. The right beliefs will maximize your potential; the wrong ones will limit it, thereby minimizing your effectiveness.

Why do we tolerate wrong beliefs in the first place? Why not change them and enjoy a better life? The answer: We invest more in our beliefs than we realize. Therefore, changing them is difficult—even harder than changing our behavior or environment. But if we are determined to understand our beliefs and remain open to adjusting them, the rewards are fantastic! Once our beliefs change, our behavior and environment can change, too.

I wish that this would happen more than it does. After more than four decades in the business of helping others, I can say that my biggest challenge involves people's inability or unwillingness to rethink their beliefs. The "calcification" of ideas can taint one's perception of life's most important issues. It can also cause someone to dig in his heels over the most insignificant matters, at great cost to his marriage, career, reputation, and so forth.

Which beliefs do you defend the most adamantly? Are you sure you are invested in them for the right reasons? Is being right more important to you than respecting others? Is driving an impressive automobile so important that you rationalize being up to your eyeballs in debt? Where has your adamant defense of these beliefs taken you?

If you desire to see change happen, or if you are aware that certain areas of your life are chronically out of alignment, all you really need is to make yourself teachable. Find out whether you are holding on to beliefs that are less than the whole truth. If you are, let them go.

Identity

Simply put, identity is a structure involving two key elements: who you are and what you stand for. These two elements are so inseparable that if you do anything out of sync with what you stand for, you will feel as if you have betrayed your own self.

Like all the structures we have already discussed in this chapter, identity taps into and affects all the others. But your identity is closely attached to another important feature: your destiny. The two cannot be separated. Who you are and what you were created to do are virtually one and the same. Knowing one means knowing the other.

Knowing who you are is important, but knowing who you are *not* is also important. This is especially vital in the crucible known as the *gap*. That is the place where the person you *think you are* is most tested, and the parts of you that don't belong melt away, so that what remains is the real you—your authentic identity.

Here is how I explain identity in another book:

[Identity] is your intuitive knowledge of self. It is the deep down recognition of your place as a unique human being. It involves the understanding of your inherent worth apart from externals such as what you do and how you look. Authentic identity is at the very core of your being. It is not based on performance, although your sense of identity affects your performance. Your identity is based upon who you were created to be.[11]

You are who you are for a reason, and that reason is your destined purpose in this life. To be effective in fulfilling your purpose requires that you first understand that purpose. And the gap is a great place to iron it out. Allow the gap to distill your concepts of self. Then, watch as your authentic identity becomes clearer and your destiny is confirmed.

Realize, though, that a fresh understanding of your purpose doesn't come at the same speed that a microwave meal is cooked. There is a process involved. Don't be alarmed when your *now* doesn't seem to measure up to your destiny. Snapshots of your journey never show all that you are becoming. Yet, taking those snapshots is invaluable, and learning from them will guide you straight through the gap and beyond.

Sounding the Depths

1. Does the idea that you designed your own life stick in your craw? What do your feelings tell you?

2. Do you often find yourself feeling powerless? How is your perception of powerlessness changing, and why?

3. How does Derrick Coleman's story help to reveal how structures may be affecting your current reality?

4. As you read through this chapter, what habitual perceptions came to mind? How do you suppose these perceptions were formed?

5. Which structures from Dilts's model speak the most clearly to your life? What about them is most significant in your experience?

Notes

1. Derrick Coleman's story is from "The Sound of Silence in the NFL," NFL. com, "Seattle Seahawks," December 14, 2013, http://www.nfl.com/videos/seattle-seahawks/0ap2000000297828/Derrick-Coleman-The-sound-of-silence-in-the-NFL.
2. Ibid.
3. Ibid.
4. Ibid.
5. Robert Dilts, "Modeling," The Article of the Month, NLP University, http://www.nlpu.com/Articles/artic19.htm.
6. Robert R. Dilts, *Changing Belief Systems with NLP* (Capitola, CA: Meta Publications, 1990), 12.
7. The Dilts pyramid has been used and adapted by many psychologists and thinkers. In all cases, we are indebted to Robert R. Dilts's original version.
8. Robert K. Merton, *Social Theory and Social Structure* (New York: Simon & Schuster, 1968), 477.
9. W. I. Thomas, "Definition of the Situation," excerpted from W. I. Thomas, *The Unadjusted Girl* (Boston, Little, Brown, and Co., 1923), posted at Sociosite, http://www.sociosite.net/topics/texts/thomas.php.
10. Senge, *Fifth Discipline*, 163.
11. Mark J. Chironna, *Download Your Destiny Code* (Motivational Press, Inc., 2012).

6

The Wide-awake Designer

You are reading this book for a reason. Most likely, you have hit strange new seas that you now intend to navigate. You have been studying snapshots of your life, searching for their deeper meanings. You realize that you did what most of us do: You reacted to the scenes in your story to the degree that you understood them. If it looked like success, you rejoiced and moved on. If it reeked of failure, you wrote it off as a blunder and a waste of time. And, like many of us, you are still kicking that rock of regret down the road ahead.

You know in your heart that these snapshots are never meaningless, but you may have long since given up on understanding them. Each time you dust them off, they look a little different, not because you are flighty or schizophrenic but due to the fact that both you and your perceptions are changing continuously.

Now, you are in the gap, and everything you thought you knew has been turned inside out. You are like someone with an itch that cannot be scratched. You cannot resolve the weirdness, but neither can you get it out of your mind.

You could not be in a more promising position. Your gap, if you choose to engage it, will turn things around and set them in a new light. It will help you to see yourself and your story in new, innovative ways so that you can break free from old paradigms and burst upon the life you were destined to occupy.

You are no longer the inadvertent designer of your life. You are wide-awake!

Your next steps are big. The structures in your life are about to yield important information that will support your design. The structures that cooperate with your purpose will be reinforced, while those contradictory to it will be discarded. You will no longer perceive yourself as an accident or a freak of nature. Instead, you will discover purpose in the very ways that you move through life.

And any instances of doubt—the thought that says "I can't do that here"—will go the way of the dinosaur, so that the realization "I can do this anywhere" is free to work its wonders.

Your Way of Being

Have you noticed how people live in certain ways, move in certain ways, use certain metaphors, like certain things, and relate to their world in certain ways that make them uniquely *them?*

What you have noticed is their *way of being,* or their *ontology.* Have you have ever watched a family video of yourself and been surprised by the sound of your voice or by your mannerisms? You notice the way your eyes move or the way you tilt your head. You are surprised at your way of moving and responding to others. You always pictured yourself in a certain way, but after watching the video, you realize how little you actually understand your own way of being.

Your way of being is more than how you carry yourself. It is your way of life and of knowing what you know. It is about your character, your lifestyle, and your mode of behavior. Still, it is not as much about *doing* as about *being,* and about the animating principle behind the manner in which you express who you are.

Your way of being is not static but fluid. It responds to changes in perception that continually redefine your understanding of reality. Certain things about you have always been there, yet your current way of being is not entirely the same as it was when you were five years old. You have more information and more "water under the bridge." Your way of being—your *ontology*—has evolved.

A key component of your ontology is the way you fit with the world around you. Notice that I did not say "fit *in*"; I said "fit *with*." We will take a closer look at this concept later. For now, just recognize that the way you *fit with the world* is an important component of your way of being.

Way of Being and Interpreting

You are a walking, talking set of observations and interpretations. In chapter 5, we recognized the connection between your perceptions and your conceptions. You know that you are a meaning-maker. You perceive and interpret the signs, symbols, and metaphors that show up in your environment, and your interpretations are directly linked to your habits of perception.

In other words, you continuously ingest and digest information from the world around you (and from your own thought processes). You then filter this information through your habitual ways of seeing the world, and your interpretations produce your working reality.

The staffer who describes his job as a "war zone" is not only reflecting the nature of his workplace; he is also revealing his way of seeing his world. No one likes a war zone, but civilian employees surely don't expect to work in one. Therefore, the metaphor reveals a professional environment that the staffer views as being virtually unbearable.

But how consciously aware is the staffer who uses this metaphor? How accurate is the assessment? The answers to these questions are important if you want to become a wide-awake designer. Perceptions and interpretations *must* be considered consciously in order for your design to work. That means you must scrutinize your perceptions. Is your workplace really a war zone? Or do your fears cause you to habitually perceive relationships as battles to be fought?

What if you discarded the war zone metaphor and the bunker mentality it reveals? What if you saw your job as a place (admittedly, an imperfect one) where "give and take" replaces "my way or the highway"? Suddenly, your workplace becomes a classroom in which you can learn to communicate at a more constructive level. Cooperation and compassion replace fear and loathing. No longer do you show up armed to the emotional teeth, viewing everyone as "the enemy." And no longer do you clock out so drained by contention that your home becomes your next theater of battle.

You are the interpreter of the signs you see. You don't interpret them exactly the same way the next guy would. Imagine that your coworker Tom is a combat veteran. Having experienced multiple tours of duty in actual war zones, he considers the term much more than a metaphor. A war zone was his literal workplace, and it did not look anything like the place where you both work now. Tom's metaphor for the office might be "a piece of cake."

Again, your interpretations are formed by your way of being, which includes:

+ Your habits of perception (how you see your world)

+ Your experiences (based on your perceptions)

+ The conceptions that are formed from your perceptions (the "rules" you make based on what you see or think you see)

Your interpretations are based on the past, yet they impact your future. To become a wide-awake designer of your life, you must interpret consciously.

Leave the Past Where It Belongs

Do you react to certain words or situations in alarming ways? Are you peaceful one moment and in turmoil the next? Do certain people know just how and when to press your buttons?

We all have "buttons." Some are perfectly reasonable and appropriate reactions to obscene or brutal acts. If you witness a murder, you *should* experience a flood of emotion. What I am talking about here are lingering symptoms from past distresses—triggers that fire unexpectedly when a memory is stirred by a new circumstance.

Because these memories are often buried, our reactions to them are usually unconscious. We may not realize that they are connected to the past. Latent distresses simmer in secret, but our responses occur in plain sight. "Old news" taints our interpretations of signs and symbols and causes reactions that are sometimes inexplicable and out of proportion.

These symptoms of past distresses confirm the buried memories that are perpetuating negative patterns in our lives. To the degree that they remain buried, we have not crossed the threshold between the conscious and unconscious realms.

In chapter 4, we saw how metaphorical pilgrimage takes us to the threshold where most gap navigation takes place. If we remain willing to explore it, we can make the connection between what is happening "above the water" and what remains hidden beneath the surface.

Radio talk-show host Dave Ramsey touched on this connection during an on-air conversation with a listener. The woman explained that her husband adamantly believed married couples should not establish joint finances. She was uncomfortable with this idea and asked Ramsey for his opinion.

He was equally skeptical and went on to explain the potential ramifications to the couple's financial future. Trying to find the root of the issue, Ramsey asked the woman whether her husband had ever been married before. She replied that he had not. Ramsey then asked whether his parents had been divorced. She answered that they had.

Bingo! Ramsey had found the trigger. The husband's father had warned him against joint finances. The older man's conception was based on his perceptions of his own failed marriage. As far as he could tell, having joint finances was connected with getting divorced. His son had accepted his evaluation.[1] In reality, the father was projecting: he saw marriage not as it was but as *he* was.

Past memories had produced the older man's current symptoms. And because his son also had painful memories of the divorce, the symptom was shared. So, whenever the wife of the younger man urged her husband to streamline their finances, he became defensive. He probably thought he was simply reacting to her request. But her request was not the issue. The problem was a past memory that was stirring fresh reactions as long as it remained buried in his unconscious mind.

Becoming aware of hidden memories is critical to preventing recurring symptoms. It is a matter of crossing the threshold between the conscious and unconscious mind. Each time you navigate this gap, you unhook another lie and gain the freedom to make healthier choices.

That, dear navigator, is a very big deal.

Think about the last time you were triggered. What did the symptoms look like? What can you learn from them? What memory fueled your distress? How might you view the past event differently from now on?

Unhook Self-Sabotage

Self-sabotage is another sign that the threshold between the conscious mind and the unconscious mind needs to be crossed. The term sounds serious, and it is. But you don't have to be a card-carrying masochist to sabotage yourself. Most people have worked against their own self-interests in some way. Many undermine themselves routinely. Still, the issue is often undiagnosed or ignored.

Have you ever asked yourself, *Why is this happening again?* (Most of us would probably say yes.) If so, there is some aspect of self-sabotage working in your life. The first step to avoiding future damage is to admit that the pattern exists. The next step is to identify the common denominator in the pattern: *you.*

For example, let's say that you desire to marry and start a family, but your past is littered with a string of romantic relationships that exploded the moment they became "serious." Instead of rationalizing your past, examine the pattern. Are you usually the one who pulls the trigger? Or do you drive prospective marriage partners away? Do you talk about making plans for the future but withdraw in the present? Do you hear yourself repeating excuses, such as "It's not you; it's me," or "You just don't understand me"?

Legitimate red flags in your relationships should never be ignored. But sabotaging relationships because of unfinished business in your unconscious is something else entirely. It reveals a structure or structures that contradict purpose—in this case, the desire to settle down and raise a family.

The conflict is obvious: You *want* to find a mate, but you keep finding ways *not* to marry. You might be rejecting others to avoid being rejected yourself. In that case, the offending structure is the unconscious expectation of rejection. Or maybe you were raised in a broken home and fear "failing," as your parents did. So, instead of risking a divorce, you blow up your current relationship before marriage is possible, making divorce impossible.

If you continue in self-sabotage, the only life you will design is a thwarted one. The process is unconscious yet exhausting: You build your stated dream with one hand and demolish it with the other.

The solution is to navigate the threshold between your conscious mind and your unconscious mind in order to find whatever is operating there and acknowledge your part creating in the pattern. Admit that you are achieving outcomes that are opposite to the ones you say you want. Own the opportunity to grow. Ask yourself: What mistaken belief fuels this situation? What unfinished business is holding me back? Do I fear rejection or failure? Do I see myself as being unworthy of love or incapable of a healthy relationship? And if so, how can I correct my perceptions?

There is an important caveat here: I am not suggesting that you discount your reactions. They are not trivial. Your beliefs and your behavior may have been formed around real experiences that caused lasting pain. If rejection was the culprit, your profound fear of being rejected is understandable. Yet two ideas must also be understood: (1) Because fear operates at the unconscious level, it controls you and everything you touch; and (2) Fear has no business being your master.

There is another important point to consider: Those who have suffered rejection often see acceptance as an even greater threat. This might seem counterintuitive, but it is logical. Rejection can become familiar territory (i.e., the devil you know). When this happens, acceptance (and the intimacy it produces) seems alien and even dangerous. Fear, then, becomes preemptive, striking out against the possibility of intimacy.

Do you see how self-sabotage works? The real enemy is not "out there." It is hidden in faulty structures that express *self* in unhealthy ways.

Expose the Faulty Belief That Says, "I Can't Do That Here"

Structures that contradict purpose always inform us of what we *cannot* do. Because these structures function at the unconscious level, we buy into the "I can't" premise and adopt its language. This is especially true when our losses are recurring. We capture our outcomes in words that convey our sense of inevitability:

Nothing will ever change.

It's always one step forward and two steps back.

My boss won't promote me because she's jealous of me.

People don't accept me because I grew up on the wrong side of the tracks.

Such expressions not only reflect our beliefs; they also justify them. This is how millions of people end up taking their unspent potential to their graves. They regret their unfulfilled dreams, yet they fail to understand what went wrong.

Others escape this fate by connecting the dots before it's too late. They recognize the patterns in their lives and dare to venture outside the box. They don't allow themselves to be hemmed in by their fears or by people who say, "You should do this"; "You ought to do that"; "You must go there"; "You don't belong here."

Playing to your fears, or the expectations of others, is a losing hand. It evokes a sense of impossibility that is unfounded yet powerfully destructive. It can keep you locked out of your own life and train you to see yourself in radically distorted ways. It can inspire decisions that ratify the lie you have swallowed. And, as always, the mind-set comes down to five forbidding words: *I can't do that here.*

This is the self-fulfilling prophecy of inadvertent designers. But you are no longer in their ranks. You have entered the realm of wide-awake, powerful dreamers. Whatever damage your "I can't" has already caused is behind you. Now it is time to understand where the idea came from, so you can put it to rest, once and for all!

The Structure of "I Can't Do That Here"

What poses as a statement of physical reality is really much more than that. It is the verbalization of habitual and complex perceptions of the world and your place in it. "I can't do that here" is a statement closely connected to your way of being. Therefore, it can be reverse engineered to uncover the layers of structure hidden beneath it.

I don't know anyone who has never uttered or believed those five words. Of course, they can be conveyed in many ways. But the bottom line remains the same. See if you can relate to any of the versions of "I can't do that here" listed below:

When our nest egg is big enough, I'll be able to spend more time with my family.

When I find a husband, I'll be happy.

When my wife quits bugging me, I'll treat her better.

If I had a better boss, I could succeed at work.

Are certain statements from your past ringing in your ears? You can see that some interpretations of "I can't do that here" are more blatant than others, but all of them say essentially the same thing: "I want to accomplish a certain thing, but my circumstances prevent me from doing so." It sounds logical enough, and there might even be a grain of truth in it. Yet the limitations are mostly self-imposed. They come from flawed beliefs—not random ideas but ones that took shape in response to real experiences or to situations that we perceived to be real.

Now, let's go back to the essential statement—"I can't do that here." The diagram below shows how each part of it connects with five of Robert Dilts's neurological levels.[2]

When you say, "I can't do that here," you believe it is absolutely true. Your conviction, however, does not make the statement accurate. Your sincerity simply proves that you perceive it to be so. Notice, too, that the statement is not a simple negation. It might seem straightforward to say, "I can't do a certain thing in a certain place," but the assertion reveals a blend of structures, including the following:

+ Aspects of the speaker's sense of identity ("*I am* somehow 'smaller' than the situation at hand.")

+ Insight into the speaker's belief system ("*I believe* this is impossible.")

+ An estimation of personal ability ("*I cannot* complete *that* activity/objective/behavior.")

+ A sense of what is appropriate or achievable here ("*That* task/objective/behavior *cannot* happen here.")

+ A sense that the environment is constraining ("*This environment* is working against *that* task/objective/behavior.")

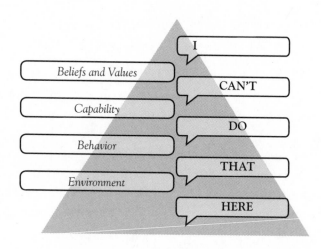

(Reproduced with permission of the author.
Copyright © 1998 by Robert Dilts, Santa Cruz, CA)

Can you identify an "I can't do that here" situation in your life? Is there one that seems to be stalking you? Take a few moments to identify and unpack any that come to mind. Consider their real meaning, as we did above, then follow them to their logical conclusions. Can you see how they are playing out?

Reality is influenced and shaped not from without but from within. Even when wrong attitudes and poor choices seem to limit your options, there are more avenues to consider. Every journey has its exodus events, including yours. Just as the Israelite slaves exited Egypt and were changed, your exodus events will liberate you from faded, self-limiting ideas. Allow the possibilities to emerge, and the impossibility that once seemed inevitable will evaporate.

An Example Close to Home

My wife, Ruth, and I have been blessed with two amazing sons. The older is Matthew, a kinesthetic, or hands-on, learner. He is as smart as a whip, and yet, from grade school through college, he struggled with math. Matthew had to work harder preparing for tests than did many of his classmates. Despite his efforts, his performance on tests was uneven.

The struggle created frustration for Matthew and his teachers, some of whom scolded him for scoring poorly. Their reactions conveyed a damaging message: *When it comes to math, you are incapable.* These teachers did not address my son at the level of his behavior. Instead, they maligned his capability. Addressing a poor test performance would have been one thing; declaring Matthew "incapable" was another matter.

Capability is more closely related to identity than behavior is. So, in Matthew's case, a poor performance became a source of shame. Instead of evaluating what Matthew had done, certain teachers demeaned who he was. The effect was profound, and the structure it created distorted reality. *I didn't do well on my test* morphed into *I didn't do well because I am incapable of doing well; and if I am incapable of doing well, there must be something wrong with me.*

The great irony is that my son grasps math at the cellular level. He is an amazing percussionist. He could not do what he does without understanding mathematics. Ask him to play a series of quarter-note triplets followed by a series of dotted eighths and sixteenth notes in pairs of four, and Matthew doesn't have to stop to figure it out. He just plays it. He struggled with algebraic equations, yet he *feels* math, and he helps other people feel it, too.

Ruth and I delight in witnessing Matthew's journey. We have watched him reach the place of being comfortable in his own skin. His sense of identity has matured. He has overcome the labels that once caused him pain. We know that it could have turned out differently. If Matthew had accepted the label of "incapable," he might have felt justified in saying, "I can't do this here, because *I am incapable.*"

What a loss that would have been—for everyone! Thankfully, Matthew's struggle did not define him. He acknowledged his battle with test performance, and he did his best to improve his results. But he did not confuse performance with identity. As a result, he is free to use his gift to both express his identity and bring joy to others. When he sits behind his drum kit, it's to everybody's gain. Our son is a living demonstration of someone who said, "I *can* do that here!"

Everything Begins with a Thought

Nothing happens unless a thought starts it. Inadvertent designers do not recognize this rule, but they still experience its effects. Wide-awake designers consciously embrace the rule and work it to their advantage.

My son's story is a testament to the power of thoughts. Some days, he returned from school plagued by the idea that he was incapable. Fortunately, he learned not to accept these opinions as gospel truth. Instead, he actively monitored and restructured his thoughts. He refused to embody the negative suggestions he heard, and he chose to frame a future based upon the truth about him.

Thought assessment and management is a critical process for all of us. For better or worse, our thoughts govern our lives. In fact, they are the seedbed of all we do. Our thoughts and actions are inseparable. Our *doing* never happens apart from our *thinking*.

Theoretical physicist David Bohm explained the inseparability of thoughts from our actions:

The general tacit assumption in thought is that it's just telling you the way things are and that is not doing anything—that "you" are inside there, deciding what to do with the information. But you don't decide what to do with the information....Thought runs you. Thought, however, gives the false information that you are running it, that you are the one who controls thought, whereas actually thought is the one which controls each one of us.... Thought is creating divisions out of itself and then saying that they are there naturally.[3]

Bohm applies this concept at the level of national affairs. He explains that divisions among nations (and all forms of division) don't just happen; they begin in people's thoughts. And he believes this is largely an unconscious process. We think about our outcomes but then fail to realize that our outcomes originated in our thinking.

This is another major feature of thought: *thought doesn't know it is doing something and then it struggles against what it is doing.* It doesn't want to know that it is doing it. And it struggles against the results, trying to avoid those unpleasant results while keeping on with the way of thinking. That is what I call *sustained* incoherence.[4]

According to Bohm, thoughts can never be perfectly complete; therefore, incoherence is a fact of life. Sustained incoherence is not inevitable, however. We can choose it or reject it. When life turns out differently than we expected, it would seem natural to revise our thoughts. Yet we are least willing to change our thinking when it matters most. Because we are especially invested in certain beliefs, we refuse to change our minds. As a result, we opt for incoherence—not consciously, but in response to our inner conflict.[5]

Sustained incoherence is the enemy of wide-awake designers. If you want to design a fulfilling life, you must be willing to master your thoughts.

Start Where You Are

Designing almost always involves redesigning. Even when we achieve our dreams, there are new tweaks to be made. The process of assessing where we are and then moving forward is ongoing.

At every stage, an accurate assessment of our current reality is important if we are to master our thoughts and engage in wide-awake designing. The key is to be honest about where you are *and* how you feel about it. Denying the rough patches, or stifling your feelings about them, will only guarantee stagnancy and deterioration. But being honest with yourself takes more than refusing to lie. Owning the truth means seeing the design of your life structure as it is, warts and all. It might not be pretty, but your redesign process must start precisely where you are. In cannot start where you would like to be.

As you begin the redesign process, remember to remain conscious of your thoughts. Like my son Matthew, you might be labeled as "incapable" in some area. Examine that assessment. Be realistic, but never let anyone else's negative thoughts (or your own negative thoughts, for that matter) determine your outcomes. If you cannot carry a tune, your prospects of singing with the Metropolitan Opera are slim to none. Yet that is not the end of the world for you. It simply means that your capabilities lie elsewhere.

Examine the entire structure of your life. Find the truth about who you are—and who you are not—and then run with it. Don't blame your environment or your zip code. Don't blame your upbringing or your education. Drop the blame game. It never motivated anyone to achieve greatness. If you are tempted to blame others, find the source of shame behind that urge. If blame and shame have you bound, reach out to a competent counselor. You are not under a life sentence; with a little help, you can get past these issues.

Ask Yourself the Right Questions

Unmastered thoughts have a life of their own. If your mind has ever wandered, you know how uncontrolled your thoughts can be. However, they can be made to serve you better. Knowing how much power your thoughts have is a great start. Directing them in more productive ways is an essential skill of wide-awake designers.

One of the best ways to corral your thoughts is to ask yourself questions designed to unpack their real meanings. The neurological levels of Robert Dilts's pyramid provide the perfect framework for your "questionnaire." According to Dilts and others, each level provokes questioning that

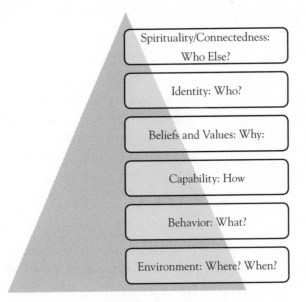

Spirituality/Connectedness:
Who Else?

Identity: Who?

Beliefs and Values: Why:

Capability: How

Behavior: What?

Environment: Where? When?

can reveal both structure and purpose.

The questions are the same ones any investigator or storyteller would use: *Who? What? When? Where? Why?* and *How?* (albeit in a different order). The diagram below connects the questions to their corresponding neurological level.[6]

(Reproduced with permission of the author.
Copyright © 1998 by Robert Dilts, Santa Cruz, CA)

Where? When?

Starting at the bottom of the pyramid, the first questions are prompted by your environment; as such, they are meant to help tune your awareness to the resources that are already available around you. Regardless of how you view your environment, it contains resources, just like every other environment. The question is where those resources are and whether they show up when you think they should. Asking the right questions will help you to adjust your perspectives and perceptions to make the most of your environment.

It is important to keep in mind that your available resources might not look the way you expect them to. Even the absence of a certain resource can be become an opportunity. If it's not there, you can decide to become a supplier!

What?

This question points you in the direction of behaviors that are most conducive to your environment and most compatible with your purpose. What are you doing? What should you be doing? What could you be doing better? If you live near a large retirement community and want to serve the elderly, offering bungee-jumping lessons might not be the best choice. But if you offer to help the elderly with painting or landscaping, opportunities will abound.

How?

This question—how to accomplish your purpose and how best to use your capabilities—will help you assess your gifts in realistic ways. The answers you get will speak to every part of you—the parts that are well developed, underdeveloped, or even missing in action. Asking *how* will help you direct your capabilities toward fruitful endeavors rather than rabbit trails. When you hit a barrier, asking *How?* will spark creative solutions and innovations that better serve you and others. Solving the *how* will help you write a more satisfying life story.

Why?

Whenever you answer this question, you tap into what matters most. Your beliefs and values determine your *why*, even when you are not consciously aware of what your beliefs and values are. Asking *Why?* takes you to the threshold between your conscious and unconscious mind. Therefore, it keeps you from living on autopilot and gives you a deeper understanding of your story. When you understand the *why* behind the choices you habitually make, the mystery of the patterns in your life will be solved, and you will be free to redesign.

Who?

This question is intrinsically human. We sometimes ask the questions "Who am I?" or "Who is this person to me?" in a rhetorical sense, as though the questions are more important than the answers. But the answers are critical to our sense of self. At its deepest levels, identity is tied to destiny, purpose, passion, and posture in life. Knowing who we are, and who others are to us, can answer many questions we never dared to ask.

Who Else?

This final question cuts to the core of your spirituality, as well as to your connectedness to others and to the world around you. It reveals two concurrent truths: (1) No human being is isolated; and (2) The world does not revolve around self. Neurologically speaking, you were not wired to live in a *me*-centered world but in a *"we"* world.[7] Your purpose involves other people. Wherever you go and whatever you do, you will need to answer the question *Who else?*

Design and Live Every Level

Each neurological level is packed with power that we cannot afford to underestimate or ignore. From our environment to our spirituality, there is the miracle of being human, the responsibility in being uniquely gifted, the blessing of being part of a larger community and a broader scheme, and the absolute wonder of a greater purpose that compels us to dream—and to fulfill those dreams.

I dare you to design and live at every level. Understand your environment and draw from it what you need. Know what you believe, and if you discover that you have believed amiss, be willing to change your mind. Use your gifts. Find what's important. Connect with those whom you are called to serve and study. Question eternal matters. Act in ways that defy self-imposed limits and the unfair expectations of others.

Navigate the waters, wherever they lead, and cross every gap that opens up before you. You can rest assured that this kind of journey will take you where you have longed in your heart of hearts to go—to a place that affirms your significance and promotes the fullest expression of it.

Sounding the Depths

1. Explain, in your own words, why your individual perceptions are so important. Explain how a habitual perception has formed a metaphor you use (i.e., "If I didn't have bad news, I'd have no news at all," or "I'm the black sheep of my family," or "I am the apple of my father's eye.")

2. In your life, what recurring symptoms of distress are the most apparent?

3. Find one pattern in your life that points to possible self-sabotage. Is this your first awareness of it? How does the realization change your paradigm?

4. Select one neurological level and its corresponding piece of the statement "I can't do that here." Then, relate it to your life experience.

5. How does the bringing of unconscious thoughts to your conscious reality help explain where you are now?

Notes

1. *The Dave Ramsey Show*, February 11, 2014.
2. The Dilts pyramid has been used and adapted by many psychologists and other thinkers. In all cases, we are indebted to Robert R. Dilts's original version.
3. David Bohm, *Thought as a System* (London: Routledge, 1994), 5–6.
4. Ibid., 11.
5. Ibid.
6. This is another adaption of the Dilts pyramid.
7. Daniel J. Siegel, M.D., *Mindsight: The New Science of Personal Transformation* (New York: Bantam Books, 2011), 10.

7

Alive on the Threshold

Encased in special gear, and with the whole world watching, daredevil Felix Baumgartner stood on the edge of space and history. After five years of intensive preparation, he stepped from his "porch" in the stratosphere and plunged earthward.[1] Twenty-four miles later, he'd torn up the record books. Baumgartner broke the sound barrier *without a vehicle* and landed safely in Roswell, New Mexico.

The mission was precision-planned. Still, there were no guarantees, and Baumgartner knew it. He quoted the saying, "A risk-free flight never leaves the ground."[2] He knew what every history-maker knows: Greatness has a price tag. He had counted the cost and decided—not whimsically or from realms of denial—that he would pursue his mission, despite the risks.

Baumgartner was no stranger to danger. As a skydiver and a BASE jumper, he considered parachutes among his closest companions. He'd done it all and had his share of close calls. And his experiences led him to October 14, 2012—the day of his ultimate jump. If he succeeded, he would own a place in history, and his team's innovations would serve the space exploration community for generations to come. If the mission failed, Baumgartner might not live to regret it.

The trip to earth was spectacular, but it was only a part of Baumgartner's journey. Long before he arrived in the stratosphere, an inner pilgrimage had been made. He'd had to wrestle with every structure that stood in contradiction to his destiny. And with a story as cutting-edge as Baumgartner's, the opposition had to have been fierce.

One structure nearly took Baumgartner down. It was one he'd thought he had mastered: *fear.*

In an interview with CNN, he said:

Fear has become a friend of mine....It's what prevents me from stepping too far over the line. On a mission like this, you need to be mentally fit and have total control over what you do, and I'm preparing very thoroughly.[3]

But his plan to break the unofficial record, set in 1960 by retired Col. Joe Kittinger with a leap from 102,800 feet, revealed a fear that Baumgartner hadn't felt before.[4]

The new face of fear was claustrophobia. Baumgartner's pressurized suit virtually entombed him, so restricting his movement that he experienced panic attacks. His team understood the implications to the mission and enlisted help. They brought in psychologist Dr. Michael Gervais, who works with extreme athletes. Gervais helped Baumgartner explore and ultimately cross the threshold between his unconscious and unconscious mind.

[The suit] was a symbol of [Baumgartner's] not having complete control of the situation. To combat this, Gervais said, Baumgartner had to reconnect with his vision. He'd become too focused on the suit, not the goal he hoped to reach wearing it....To reconnect with his vision, Baumgartner needed to reconnect to what Gervais called his hidden journey—what the jump meant to him, beyond being the first person to skydive from so great a height, or being the first person to exceed the speed of sound (about 700 mph at that altitude) in free fall. The hidden journey, he said, is much more basic: Baumgartner wants to go somewhere no one has ever been.

Gervais taught Baumgartner how to better manage his mind and body under pressure.[5]

The pressurized suit was designed to keep the space jumper alive; yet, on an unconscious level, it symbolized a different kind of danger. Gervais knew that Baumgartner's success hinged on his thoughts being rewired. So, he guided the jumper through many panic-producing situations until Baumgartner was consistently able to face his fear and overcome it.

In a very real sense, Baumgartner's newfound fear was his final obstacle. Having cleared it from his path, he was free to approach the threshold—of his jump and of his destiny—fully alive.

> Have new vistas revealed previously undetected fears to you? How can your larger perspective help you overcome your fear?

Good-bye, Business as Usual

As I mentioned earlier, the seam between the conscious and unconscious realms is called the *liminal space*. Whether or not we realize it, we brush against this space every day—and routinely avoid it. Most often, we find it too ethereal or daunting to contemplate. So, we back away, later to wonder why our progress has been meager.

Felix Baumgartner's dream was too far-out and far-reaching for him to treat even routine matters with a "business as usual" approach. The liminal space had to be faced, and every brush with it was a head-on collision. He had bet the farm on a mission that had become consequential to many. The stakes were high, and hiding was not an option. He could not cross from the stratosphere to the New Mexican desert until he had crossed the liminal space within.

Ecumenical teacher Richard Rohr explains this inner space in an overtly spiritual context, yet his point about "chronic liminality" applies to all great achievers:

Nothing good or creative emerges from business as usual. Much of the work of the God of the Bible is to get people into liminal space, and to keep them there long enough so they can learn something essential. It is the ultimate teachable space, maybe the only one. Most spiritual giants try to live lives of "chronic liminality" in some sense. They know it is the only position that insures ongoing wisdom, broader perspective and ever-deeper compassion. The Jewish prophets, Socrates and Diogenes, Jesus, Francis, Buddha, Gandhi, virgins and hermitesses, the Hindu sanyassi, the Native shamans immediately come to mind.[6]

Chronic liminality is the lifestyle of those who reject the security of the comfort zone. These "liminars" move from threshold to threshold, always learning to see with "new eyes." They don't lay down roots in places where their emotions will be soothed. They pursue milestones that force them to the edge. When the mission is accomplished, they break camp and head for the next gap. Instead of being controlled by contradicting structures, liminars consciously become single-eyed. In other words, their focus on the vision forces all distractions out of view.

This is what Baumgartner did when claustrophobia threatened his mission. He returned to the vision and reconnected with his purpose. The idea of doing what no one else had ever done took center stage again. Therefore, fear had to step aside. Because he had made what Dr. Michael Gervais called the "hidden journey," Baumgartner's outer journey could not be hindered.

Identifying the Threshold

The threshold of every physical and metaphorical pilgrimage is the liminal space. When we arrive there, we discover its daunting logistics. How could it be any other way? How could we ever be perfectly prepared to cross a previously unknown place? The truth is that we cannot. We are so ill-equipped that we come to the place possessing nothing—at least, nothing that seems to be of value.

British evangelist T. Austin Sparks explained this phenomenon in the context of the spiritual journey. His idea speaks to every sojourner, whether spiritually-minded or not: "When, therefore, we have faced that fact, and have recognized its implications, we shall see that here is a land, which is locked up, into which we cannot enter, and for which we have no equipment."[7]

The liminal space forces us beyond our pat, practiced answers, because we cannot know in advance all that it will demand of us. Felix Baumgartner's entire life was a preparation for his space jump, yet even he lacked certain vital tools for his "new job." Claustrophobia had not been an obstacle in his previous endeavors. Therefore, he was forced to develop a brand-new skill.

Here's the thing: Had Baumgartner not wholly committed himself to his mission, he might never have known what was working in the dark folds of his unconscious mind. Because he held to his commitment, he underwent the process of discovery and completed the necessary follow-through. He approached the threshold, processed what he learned there, and made it work for him rather than against him.

The Essence of Threshold

Even the word *threshold* is evocative. Perhaps the most universal metaphor it conjures is that of a groom carrying his bride across the threshold of their home and into their new life together. That is the essence of *threshold*: In whatever realm, it signifies a crossing over from one place to another.

Here are just a few aspects of the threshold, with illustrations to consider:

+ **It is the starting point for a new state or experience.** When two people marry, for example, they cross over from the state of being single to the state of being one with their mate. Likewise, when an aspect of your internal landscape changes, your outer condition changes with it.

+ **It is a passageway into a new world.** The mapping of the human genome opened a passageway into the new world of genetic medicine. Likewise, the understanding of your purpose opens up a new world of destiny fulfillment.

+ **It is the lowest level at which a condition is detected.** Physical ailments are noticed when they produce enough discomfort to cross your pain threshold. This is also true of contradicting structures. They become apparent when emotional pain or frustration rises to a certain level.

+ **It is the entrance, an opening in a wall, through which you enter or leave a room or building; it is the space that a door can close.** Entrances can also be metaphorical, as in the entrance to a new career or lifestyle.

+ **It is the bottom of a doorway; it provides structural support and also supports those who pass through the doorway.** This describes the physical threshold across which a groom carries his bride, for example. Metaphorical thresholds provide support, too. Felix Baumgartner's crossing of the liminal space undergirded the success of his mission.

+ **It is the region marking a boundary.** The foothills of the Rocky Mountains are a threshold to the high country, a boundary between the desert plateau and the alpine terrain. The liminal space is a threshold that marks the boundary between your pre-threshold and post-threshold states.

+ **It is a passageway beyond the boundaries of the possible into the realm of the impossible.** In 1954, British runner Roger Bannister broke the previously impenetrable barrier of the four-minute mile. Suddenly, other athletes started doing the same. With every threshold you cross, your sense of what is possible expands.

A threshold is more than a location or structure; it is a place of profound experience in which opposition becomes opportunity. When you explore and exploit the threshold, resistance is always present. Deep in your unconscious mind, "threshold guardians" test your will and urge you to forgo transformation. They will rule until you fully commit to navigating the liminal space. Until you expose and oppose these guardians, they will continue to thwart you. As often as not, you will sense the opposition, even if you cannot pinpoint it.

thresh·old

"Also called *limen. Psychology, Physiology.* The point at which a stimulus is of sufficient intensity to begin to produce an effect: *'the threshold of consciousness; a low threshold of pain.'*"[8]

What Is Liminality, Exactly?

The Latin word *limen* refers to the threshold of a psychological or physiological response. Therefore, *liminality* is a threshold or a transitional place. This includes "the transitional period or phase of a rite of passage, during which the participant lacks social status or rank, remains anonymous, shows obedience and humility, and follows prescribed forms of conduct, dress, etc."[9]

Throughout history, rites of passage defined where one stage of life ended and the next stage began. There were clear rites of passage into adulthood and rites of passage for warriors. Rites varied from culture to culture, but they always helped the members of the tribe to understand their place in the community. Ironically, this clarity followed an interval of necessary confusion, as Barbara Miller explains:

> [L]iminality is the quality of ambiguity or disorientation that occurs in the middle stage of rituals, when participants no longer hold their pre-ritual status but have not yet begun the transition to the status they will hold when the ritual is complete. During a ritual's liminal stage, participants "stand at the threshold" between their previous way of structuring their identity, time, or community, and a new way, which the ritual establishes.[10]

Until the ritual is complete and the certificates of passage have been handed out, the liminar is betwixt and between two worlds. For example, once a single man in the tribe began the rite of passage into married life, he entered a gap between his "old life" and the one that was ahead. The rules that applied to single men no longer applied to him. Yet the standing held by married men in his culture was not yet available to him. At least temporarily, he was wedged in a *nowhere place*.

Arnold van Gennep, an early twentieth-century expert in folklore, studied this phenomenon and developed from it the seminal concept of liminality.[11] By observing tribal cultures such as that of the African Maasai, he learned how societies conceptualized transitions from one state and status into another. His work is now universally regarded, but because his expertise was in folklore studies, most of his contemporaries dismissed it. In time, however, his findings revolutionized modern views of reality. They continue to be among the most cited by psychologists, theologians, and philosophers studying liminality.

Van Gennep's studies also reveal the loss of our tribal roots and of historic rites of passage. Today, the transition into adulthood is undefined. Thirty is becoming "the new eighteen"; couples are marrying and starting families much later than they did in decades past. The formerly well-defined liminal spaces that challenged individuals and communities to move from one boundary to the next are disappearing.

There are exceptions and hints of a returning tribalism in the twenty-first century. From street gangs to the California computer-geek scene, tribal rites are evident. Street gangs have clear initiation and other rites. While they are often violent and antisocial, these rituals draw from tribal culture. In less intimidating ways, some Silicon Valley firms are organizing along tribal lines. Some have developed on-site housing—a new-millennium form of communal living that caters to the distinctive needs of techies.[12]

Every tribe adopts expectations and creeds that must be met for membership qualification. In order to belong and participate, members must complete these rituals. Regardless of how formal or informal the setting is, "tests"—both conscious and unconscious—must be passed. The street gang member must perform whatever high-risk act the tribe assigns. Until he or she does, the gang withholds standing and authority with the group. On a less overt level, Silicon Valley geeks have to embrace being connected to their coworkers seven days a week, twenty-four hours a day. That means accepting diminished privacy and a blurring of the lines between their personal and professional lives.

Liminality at Large

Cultural anthropologist Victor Turner praised Arnold van Gennep's discovery of liminality as "a major innovative, transformative dimension of the social."[13] Turner expanded the idea, saying that liminality is not limited to traditional rites of passage.[14] Instead, it is a part of everyday life.

Turner described liminality as revolutionary, having broad impact in "all phases of decisive cultural change," and creating an environment in which social roles are inverted and new ways of thinking and being become "possible and desirable."[15] Instead of preserving traditional forms of authority (what Brueggemann calls "the trustful truth of the tribe"[16]), the limina that mark all of history also produce divisions that challenge norms and cause new realities to emerge.[17]

For Turner, liminality is not just transition; it is potentiality—both what is "going to be" and "what may be."[18] Recall that pilgrimage, in earlier centuries, was the great liminal experience in the life of faith. It involved journeying to the "thin places" where miracles have occurred, are occurring now, and will occur in the future—places brimming with potential!

Liminal places appear in ordinary life, during pilgrimage, and in the midst of rites of passage. When these thresholds are crossed, the life of the liminar is irrevocably changed. But being alive on the threshold applies to communities and cultures, too. When groups cross thresholds, society is transformed. Transformations in recent decades have included the American Civil Rights movement, the movement of women into the full-time workplace, the end of apartheid in South Africa, the fall of the Berlin Wall, and countless other societal shifts.

Rites of Transition

Rites of passage are rites of transition. They are part of the human learning curve and of fulfilling one's potential. Tribes addressed their children's naiveté with rituals. They were not born understanding how dangerous their world was. Therefore, the transition to adulthood came with a prerequisite: They had to participate in acts that revealed life's razor-sharp edges. This educational process married the acknowledgment of adulthood with the sobering realization that adults meet their responsibilities in the midst of trouble, opposition, and sorrow. Young tribal members were not qualified to carry on the tribe's legacy until they had made this vital transition.

Thresholds crossed outside the arena of formal rituals serve the same purpose. When younger people face new paradigms—the death of a young friend, the responsibilities of parenting, or the betrayal of a confidant—they learn to contend with the ambiguities of right and wrong, of good and evil. Before they "came of age," they were largely protected from issues of great magnitude. But life forces young liminars to grasp these matters. How else will they succeed in life or learn to protect their own children? Unless they cross difficult thresholds, they cannot.

The lessons learned in our liminal spaces are not always about things we have not seen before. Often, they are about things we have seen but had not previously noticed. Have you ever returned to a book, movie, or TV program a second or third time and found something new? I know I have. No matter how many times I go back, something else stands out. I now understand that I cannot really "see" things that I haven't yet experienced.

For example, if I watched *The Waltons* during my youth, I would have seen the stories from a youth's perspective. If I watched the show again a dozen years ago, I would have keyed into the parents' side of the story. Watching it today, I would especially notice Grandpa's part in the story.

Rites of passage help to illuminate things that may have been seen but not yet learned by experience. These transitions allow us to see with new eyes, as though witnessing a bringing out from the shadows something that was already under our noses. Things that must be known in the next phase of life suddenly become real and meaningful—not necessarily in a single moment, but in phases.

Has a recent transition helped you to see your world with new eyes? How so?

The Phases of Passage

Phase 1: Separation/Preliminary Phase

The first phase of a rite of passage is the separation, or the preliminary phase. The etymology of the word *preliminary* provides hints about the nature of this phase. The *Online Etymology Dictionary* explains it this way:

Preliminary (adj.): 1660s, from French *préliminaire* and directly from Medieval Latin *praeliminaris*, from Latin *prae-* "before" (see *pre-*) + *limen* (genitive *liminis*) "threshold" (see *limit* (n.)). A word that arose in reference to negotiations to end the Thirty Years' War. Earliest attested form in English is *preliminaries* (n.), 1650s.[19]

So, we see that *pre-limen* means "pre-threshold." The separation phase occurs on the near side of the threshold.

The above entry refers us to the word *limit*, so we'll take a look at its etymology, too:

> Limit (n.): c. 1400, "boundary, frontier," from Old French *limite* "a boundary," from Latin *limitem* (nominative *limes*) "a boundary, limit, border, embankment between fields," related to *limen* "threshold." Originally of territory; general sense from early 15 c. Colloquial sense of "the very extreme, the greatest degree imaginable" is from 1904.[20]

Limit clearly speaks to a border or boundary, but it comes from the same root as *preliminary*. Preliminary things always precede a main event and prepare you for it. So, in the preliminary phase, you approach the entry, or threshold, of transition.

As far as the separation aspect of this phase is concerned, an appropriate synonym would be *segregation*. This implies that you are pulled out from the aggregate (the greater whole of which you are part, such as your community). When you are segregated, you become detached from the whole, and your behavior signifies your separate state.

Here is a modern-day example of separation: You propose marriage to your sweetheart, and she accepts. You arrange a get-together with your three best buddies to announce your engagement to them. The four of you meet at a favorite sports bar. Over dinner, you share your news. When dinner is over, they plan to hit the late-night spots the four of you frequent. In the past, you would have joined them; but now you feel less inclined to go along.

You have not yet completed the transition to married life, but you are already becoming detached from your single friends. You have entered separation from the familiar state and status you had long known because you are being prepared to enter the state and status of the person you are becoming—a married man. The rules that applied in your previous state (unquestioned all-nighters with the guys) no longer apply. Yet the privileges of your upcoming state and status as a married man are not in place, either. This is the uncomfortable, ambiguous state every liminar enters. There are tests yet to be taken before you enter married life, but separation comes first.

As a college freshman, I pledged Phi Mu Alpha Sinfonia, a national music fraternity. I wanted to be a Phi Mu brother because I wanted to be around musical greats like Dave Brubeck, Duke Ellington, and others who belonged to the fraternity.

Fourteen other freshmen wanted to pledge with me. The fifteen of us agreed to the process: We would become *worms*. To become a Phi Mu brother, you had to become a worm first. No longer were we plain ole college freshman. We were worms, and we had to dress accordingly, in weird blue jackets with blue bow ties—the nerdy antithesis of 1970s fashion!

Our garb separated us from the rest of the campus population and pointed us out to the Phi Mu brothers who had been ordained to interrogate us from a prepared script:

"Pledge Worm, what time is it?" they would ask.

The answer was excruciating. "Sir, due to the failure of the inner workings of my chronometer, by which the great sidereal movements from which time is generally reckoned dictates the movement of the second hand, I cannot state the correct time; but, without fear of being too far wrong, I state the time as being approximately five minutes after two."

For seven consecutive days, we worms had to answer this and other questions the same way every time. It sounds silly and pointless, but it wasn't; it was part of our rite of passage. We wanted to pass the transition requirements, so we complied, even when it led to public embarrassment.

"Worm, give me twenty-five push-ups."

Whether the order was given in the library or in the student union, our answer was "Yes, sir." As we did our push-ups, everybody clapped and laughed. We were on display. We were separated.

Phase 2: The Liminal Phase

In this phase, the liminar enters a state of profound uncertainty where nothing that used to work works any longer. The "nothing is working" condition confirms your entrance into the gaping liminal phase.

The old "tricks of the trade" don't work here because your inner landscape has already begun its shift. Your crossing of the gap is not yet complete, but the inward changes you have already undergone have set in motion the transformation of your external life. All the parts are moving, just not in ways you can recognize right now. It is no wonder that doubt and ambiguity are persistent realities here. As the structure of the word *ambiguity* suggests, there is a sense of wandering without destination, as though you did not know whether you were coming or going.

Uncertainty cascades when nothing looks or works in familiar ways. Recall the character Dorothy from the film *The Wizard of Oz*. When she said to her dog, "Toto, I've a feeling we're not in Kansas anymore," she was verbalizing her entry into the liminal phase—a dimension that resembled no place she had ever been before. It was the nowhere between two somewheres, the hallway between where she used to be and where she was headed.

As disorienting as it is, the liminal phase is a sacred space necessary for transformation and for the fulfillment of destiny. The liminar must go there. Yet, just pushing through is not enough. Tests must be passed before you can exit the place. This is where your mind begins to think in brand-new ways—not because everything is beautiful but because the resistance is great, and you are under pressure, a salmon swimming against the current of its former life.

Don't be ashamed to ask for help. At times, you will need guidance from someone who understands the place you are in and how the psyche works there. Look for someone who is trained to help, someone who can teach you to uncover and overcome the resistances operating deep within you.

Phase 3: Aggregation

In the third and final phase of the rite of passage, the liminar is reintroduced to the social order, but with a new standing. The time of separation is done. The season of ambiguity is over, at least for now.

This is when you look back and begin to understand how far you have come. As you rejoin the tribe, you bring with you the perspective of a more seasoned "warrior." The consummation of the passage is finished. The threshold has been crossed; the gap has been navigated. You return to a more stable state, with new rights, as well as new obligations. The tribe has increased its expectations of you because you have more to offer now than you did earlier. This is a central fact of your journey: Each new state stretches you a little (or a lot) more. If it doesn't, it was either a "dead" place to begin with, or you have missed the essence of it.

That is never what your journey is about. It is about being more alive with every gap you cross. I'm not talking about appearances or forms of effervescence that impress those around you. I am talking about living fully present in the moment, with an eye to where your moment leads.

Yes…alive on every threshold!

Sounding the Depths

1. How can fear become your friend instead of your foe?

2. How can you develop or strengthen your life of "chronic liminality"? What aspects of this lifestyle either attract or repel you?

3. What "threshold guardians, if any, have you been tolerating? Can you name one challenging experience that, in retrospect, was a threshold (and an opportunity you missed)?

4. Describe a phase 1 (separation) experience that, in retrospect, served to prepare you for a new season in your life.

5. Can you relate to Dorothy's statement from *The Wizard of Oz*: "Toto, I've a feeling we're not in Kansas anymore"? Explain.

Notes

1. "World Record Jump," redbullstratos.com, http://www.redbullstratos.com/the-mission/world-record-jump/.
2. Rahim Kanani, "An Exclusive Interview with Felix Baumgartner: *National Geographic's* 2013 Adventurer of the Year," *Forbes*, November 4, 2013, http://www.forbes.com/sites/rahimkanani/2013/11/04/an-exclusive-interview-with-felix-baumgartner-national-geographics-2013-adventurer-of-the-year/.
3. Beth Carter, "How Claustrophobia Almost Grounded Supersonic Skydiver," CNN.com, October 14, 2012, http://www.cnn.com/2012/10/12/tech/claustrophobia-skydiver/index.html.
4. Ibid.
5. Ibid.
6. Richard Rohr, "Days without answers in a narrow space," NCR Online, February 1, 2002,

http://natcath.org/NCR_Online/archives2/2002a/020102/020102h.htm.
7. T. Austin Sparks, "The Stewardship of the Mystery," *The Online Library of T. Austin Sparks*, http://www.austin-sparks.net/english/books/001378.html.
8. Dictionary.com, *Dictionary.com Unabridged, Random House, Inc.*, s.v. "threshold," http://dictionary.reference.com/browse/threshold.
9. Ibid., s.v. "liminality," http://dictionary.reference.com/browse/liminality.
10. Barbara Miller, *Just the Facts 101: Textbook Key Facts–Cultural Anthropology*, 6th edition e-Study Guide (Cram 101 Publishing), http://books.google.com/books?id=LiKIcKhaq4gC&pg=PT261&lpg=PT261&dq=the+quality+of+ambiguity+or+disorientation+that+occurs+in+the+middle+stage+of+rituals&source=bl&ots=3-5PmjSm6aH&sig=SlEe3y7Ibqp_QBE-f7PvDTqBCEA&hl=en&sa=X&ei=JawCU_CYJureyAHP-ICoDw&ved=0CC0Q6AEwAQ#v=onepage&q=the%20quality%20of%20ambiguity&f=false.
11. Van Gennep's book *The Rites of Passage* continues to be a landmark work.
12. Jonathan Strickland, "How the Googleplex Works," *How Stuff Works*, http://computer.howstuffworks.com/googleplex3.htm.
13. Turner and Turner, *Image and Pilgrimage in Christian Culture*, 2.
14. Ibid.
15. Ibid.
16. Brueggemann. *David's Truth in Israel's Imagination and History*, 10.
17. Turner and Turner, *Image and Pilgrimage in Christian Culture*, 3.
18. Ibid.
19. Online Etymology Dictionary, s.v. "preliminary," http://www.etymonline.com/index.php?allowed_in_frame=0&search=preliminary&searchmode=none.
20. Ibid., s.v. "limit," http://www.etymonline.com/index.php?allowed_in_frame=0&search=limit&searchmode=none.

The Alchemy of Change

In the home where I grew up, we had huge oak trees in our backyard. They were gorgeous in the daytime, their leaves bathed in sunshine. But at bedtime, when my mom pulled down the window shade in my room, the trees morphed into something sinister.

Backlit by the moon, the window shade became a movie screen on which the waving arms of monsters danced and reached. When the wind picked up, the shadows of the tree branches reached so far that I thought they would snatch me from my bed. Their craggy, crooked hands sent chills up my spine and made sleep difficult until exhaustion would finally overtake me.

The shadowy nighttime images were deceiving. The bare outlines of something substantive suggested something baseless but captivating. I bought into the dark story, lock, stock, and barrel—until the whirling darkness left, and the shadowy figures became oak trees again.

Sinister-looking shadows still want to dance across my world, even in mature adulthood, but I know now that things are not always as they seem. In the dark, I see only outlines and suggestions. In the absence of clear sight, it is easy to accept as true what is utterly false. Even in the full light of day, I can be duped unless I look with conscious eyes.

To desire transformation is to require truth. What is true and what is false must be known. The journey is filled with clues about what is ahead. Until we embrace and understand them, we forfeit their value. The end result depends less on what the clues say than on how we interact with them. If we are willing to handle even the shadowy stuff, we will discover what we need to change, what we need to support, and what we need to disconnect.

It's a Matter of Alchemy

"Alchemy?" you ask. "Really?"

Yes, really! The word *alchemy* conjures images of strange philosophies and medieval laboratories. Yet it owns a real place in the history of hard science. It even spawned the discipline called *chemistry*.[1] The following is an excerpt from the Lloyd Library's article entitled "The History of Alchemy":

> The Indian alchemists invented steel and identified metals based on flame color. A famous woman alchemist, Maria the Jewess, from Roman Egypt introduced the use of glass apparati because it was easier to see what stage the chemicals had reached in any given process....The modern chemistry laboratory owes a great deal to the many inventions and improvements in lab equipment and processes done for the sake of alchemy.[2]

Alchemists sought nature's deep secrets and ways to use them to human advantage. One of their most passionate pursuits was a process by which to turn lead into gold. Gold was seen as the currency of power and the perfect metal. The idea of creating more of it—out of something dull and base, no less—was irresistible.

Are you getting the idea? Alchemy, for our purposes, is about turning the shadowy stuff of life into something more radiant and beneficial. This is the quest of gap navigators—those who desire to turn the secrets hidden in their thoughts and experiences into something golden.

The transformation from lead to gold is a powerful metaphor for the human dilemma. Our condition, as individuals and as a world community, is based in imperfection and alienation. We are estranged from one another and often from our divine roots. We are full of "lead" but yearn to be whole and perfect. So, we navigators become alchemists. We submit ourselves to the proving process because we know that beneath what is visible lies something more valuable than we know.

> ## al•che•my
> "A science that was used in the Middle Ages with the goal of changing ordinary metals into gold...a power or process of transforming something common into something special"[3]

Working from Shadow to Light

As we always do, we start where the red arrow is, *here* in the laboratory of life. The alchemy begins not where we wish we were but *where we are*. To begin well, we must be ruthlessly honest, not only regarding location but also regarding our belief systems and our intentions for the future. We are not looking to make cosmetic changes that feed more denial. We want to work organically, from the roots outward, so that the changes we make are genuinely for the better.

We have already searched our structures for points of contradiction. Now it is time to move beyond assessment and into transmutation. That is alchemy's purpose: "to change or alter in form, appearance, or nature and especially to a higher form."[4] We all possess set ideas about how the world works. Those ideas are based on our experiences so far. But our long-held suppositions are not enough. We must weed out any distortions in our thinking and turn them into something more functional and better aligned with our purpose.

The point is twofold: (1) to separate what is working well from what isn't, and (2) to alter the chemistry of the latter. Instead of cementing the brokenness in our lives, we are breaking up the old cement and finding the gold that is hidden in our foundation. The point is not to highlight our shortcomings or to exaggerate our strengths but to embrace objectivity and undo our misunderstandings of reality. We admit that our way of seeing will never be perfect, but it can become more objective and more productive. As long as we remain open, teachable, and coachable, our mental models will line up with where we desire to go instead of where we have been or where we fear to go.

This is not a onetime event; it is a process of lifelong learning. Where learning continues, alignment improves. When learning stops, growth ends and fragmentation returns, until life is a little more than existence, and existing becomes an acceptable choice.

Part of being teachable is never underestimating the reality and value of your past. There is power in your story—even in the suffering and pain you would rather forget. Seasons of endurance tenderize you to love and deepen your desire for wholeness and well-being.

The old shadows *can* produce fresh new fruit. You might not realize it is happening until a few words from your mouth inspire the alchemy of change in someone who hears them. The shadows that once terrified you can shed light for others to walk in!

Look Beneath the Sailboat

Do you remember our analogy of the sailboat floating on the water's surface? It was a picture of the border between the conscious and unconscious mind. We have talked about the importance of looking below the surface; but what is floating on top is important, too.

It is time to consider both. The thoughts and emotions floating atop the seam between the conscious and unconscious mind are indicators of what is buried underneath. Your role is to push past the threshold and into the liminal space—not accepting every thought and emotion that comes along but testing them all and choosing wisely. The process will blow away your projections so that you see things not as *you* are, but as *they* are. From there, you can transform invisible forms of resistance into new sources of strength and provision.

Remember that your structures are layered. Some have been operating in the background for your entire life. You might not have noticed them, but you have been living with the results they have yielded. Some structures have railroaded you and kept you stamping out the same fires, year after year. Now you know enough to connect the dots and align those deep structures so you can advance confidently toward your future.

To avoid this process is to forfeit the alchemy of change. Trying to modify any behavior without understanding its supporting structures is pointless, because behavior modification is about more than the stuff floating on the surface. Transformation happens underneath, where the trouble starts. Then your quest for meaning can reinterpret what you thought life "did" to you—and you will decide what positive use to make of it.

That is some serious navigating!

The Eye of the Beholder

Such a deep level of navigation demands objectivity. That being said, perfect objectivity is an unattainable goal for human beings. Point of view is always informed by how we see things. For example, if you were raised in a family that valued performance above all else, your expectations would reflect your upbringing. You would place high demands on others and expect even more of yourself. Even so, your habitual point of view can change. You absolutely can learn to see things more as they are and less *as you are*.

The late Dr. Maxwell Maltz was a cosmetic surgeon whose 1960 book *Psycho-Cybernetics* ignited his notoriety. In it, Maltz shared ideas designed to help people see themselves more favorably. The premise was that if you see yourself in a more positive light, the world you see becomes more favorable toward you.

Self-image and identity are central to Maltz's concept. Imagine—a man who operated on the superficial parts of people also helped readers to uncover the threshold between their conscious and unconscious thoughts! Maltz took the things he learned from his practice and applied them in broader, more consequential ways.

Two of his ideas concern us here. The first is that changing the outward appearance can change more than just a person's looks. The second is that until self-image changes, all the cosmetic surgery in the world cannot change what a patient sees in the mirror.

Two quick examples from Maltz's book prove his case. One is the story of a boy with prominent ears. He grew up being told that "he looked like a taxi-cab with both doors open. He had been ridiculed all his life—often cru-elly."[5] As a result, the boy withdrew and "became known as a moron."[6] After years of humiliation, he consulted Dr. Maltz and went under the knife. He came out with less prominent ears and an improved view of life.

The cosmetic fix solved the boy's issue. What he saw on the outside now lined up with a good self-image within. But not every patient experi-enced such a favorable outcome. Many never recovered a healthy self-image because the perceived problem with physical appearance had scarred their sense of identity. Some whose looks had been average to start with thought of themselves as ugly and imagined that their features were disturbing to others. Dr. Maltz describes such a case:

> He was a man about 40, unmarried, who held down a routine job during the day and kept himself in his room when the work day was over, never going anywhere, never doing anything. He had had many jobs and never seemed able to stay with any of them for any great length of time. His problem was that he had a rather large nose and ears that protruded a little more than is normal....He imagined that the people he came into contact with...were laugh-ing at him and talking about him behind his back....His imagin-ings grew so strong that he actually feared going out into the busi-ness world and moving among people. He hardly felt "safe," even in his home....Actually, his facial deficiencies were not serious. His nose was of the "classical Roman" type, and his ears, though some-what large, attracted no more attention than those of thousands of people with similar ears....I saw that he did not need surgery... only an understanding...that his imagination had wrought such havoc with his self-image that he had lost sight of the truth. He was not ugly.[7]

Learning to see with new eyes is vital. We'll call this being "single-eyed." It begins with your thoughts. You can see from these stories how powerfully your thoughts govern your life. They take whatever informa-tion you find and then tell you what to do with it. As a result, you become internally divided, blind to your inner struggle. Instead of making positive adjustments to your thinking, you try to smooth over the conflict. As a result, you remain paralyzed in a state of sustained incoherence. Because your thoughts and actions are inseparable, the entire fabric of your life is affected. This is how detrimental patterns can become almost intractable.

If this is your story, it can be revised going forward. You *are* invested in what you believe about yourself, and your investment *can* keep you paralyzed. But you are free to revise your beliefs. When you uncover a lie in your thinking, you are under no obligation to protect it. In fact, you ought to protect yourself—by changing your mind.

Alchemy and the Gatekeeper Between Your Ears

Lies in your thinking become stalwart threshold guardians, the gatekeepers between your ears. They test your will and easily convince you that change is unnecessary and/or impossible. They discourage you from committing to the glorious journey that you alone can take. And they tempt you to double down on stagnation, excuse-making, and self-pity.

That last statement might cause you discomfort, but it's true: Very real gatekeepers are holding the fort, and they are ruthless. They stand guard in your mind and speak doubt and fear into your heart. You are not beholden to them; but unless you are merciless in disarming them, they will keep you under submission, at their every beck and call.

The battle is absolutely unnecessary. You have the power resident within you to rule your thoughts, navigate the gap, and own the living edge of your life. After all, you have more control over your life than anyone else does. Even the threshold guardians know that. But are you using it? Or are you postponing its use and hoping that things will work themselves out?

The alchemy of change is neither mysterious nor accidental. It begins when you honor the power with which you have been entrusted—the power to change the way you see yourself and your world.

Following are some examples of surface symptoms and their underlying causes. Which ones ring your bell the loudest? Which ones do you most want to ignore? Read all of them in earnest and allow the stuff on the surface to speak to the deep inside you.

+ If you are living under the weight of shame, challenge the lie that brought shame upon you in the first place. Did an abuser blame you for the evil he or she perpetrated? That is a lie! You are not to blame for the abusive actions of others.

+ If you feel condemned for a wrong you did, own up to it and make whatever amends you can. If possible, ask for forgiveness. But don't allow your wrongdoing to become a scarlet letter that forbids you from contributing to society and doing good today.

+ If you suffer from the lingering symptoms of an old distress, such as a job layoff or broken relationship, examine your interpretation of the memory and ask yourself how you might reinterpret it. Did you assume that you deserved whatever happened, or that you had no part in the outcome? Was your interpretation accurate?

+ If your environment is distracting you from your purpose, make whatever changes are practical and helpful. If your coworker's blasting radio negatively affects your functionality and productivity, why not talk it over with him or her? But first, examine your discomfort objectively. If it is caused by a contradicting structure (such as the need to control others), your coworker might not be the problem.

+ If you keep coming up against the same barriers, take an honest inventory of any beliefs that may be limiting and weakening you rather than expanding and strengthening you. For example, if you were painfully rejected by a parent, and you find your adult relationships repeatedly ending in disaster, explore whether the *expectation* of rejection is stunting the development of your relationships.

+ If a negative self-image convinces you to withdraw from others and from the pursuit of happiness itself, carefully inspect your perceptions to determine whether they are accurate. For example, if you long to pursue a certain career, but you feel so intimidated by the prospects that you sabotage your own plans, find out what aspect of yourself you are trying to hide.

+ When you change the way you see or speak about troubling incidents, notice what happens at the level of your feelings. Is there a shift? How can you apply this information in the future? For example, if your job was cut, and you felt discarded, make the choice not to take it personally. Then pay attention to how your emotions respond to your new approach.

In each of these cases, the process of gathering information will help you to turn negatives into positives. This is the alchemy of change. The list is by no means comprehensive, but it is a good place to start. There is more than one gatekeeper between your ears. Finding them will transform your life.

Misunderstanding Failure

There is something about the word *failure* that sends us rushing for the emotional exits. No mortal human has made it through life without knowing failure. Yet we spend tremendous amounts of energy—in some cases, our whole lives—trying to deny, excuse, or hide our failures.

The fear of failure calls for some alchemy. The problem is not so much the failure itself. The real problem is what we believe about failure and how we respond to our beliefs. Our language reveals the workings of our responses and shows us what needs to change.

Right now, let's consider two common verbal responses to failure:

I am a failure.

I failed.

These expressions map out two entirely different inner landscapes. Let's say that you are an NFL placekicker who made it to the Super Bowl. With three seconds left in regulation time, the score is tied, and your team is within field goal range. You get set for the kick, knowing that if it is good, the game will end, and your team will have won. If your kick misses the mark, the game will go into overtime, and either team could win.

You do your best, but the kick is wide of the goalpost, and your team ends up losing in overtime. You can respond in two basic ways. In the first example, "I failed," you confuse your *doing* with your *being* (i.e., your performance with your essence). Since you believe that your being is to blame, you label yourself a failure. This shame-based assessment can disfigure your identity and produce even poorer performances in the future.

In the second example, "I failed," you see your failed attempt as just that—a failed attempt. You still regret it, but you do so without seeing yourself as "less than" the person you were before the kick went wide. You own your performance; you might even apologize to your teammates for having blown the scoring opportunity. But you do not punish your *being* just because your *doing* was less than perfect.

Another aspect of failure management involves your response and its effect upon your imagination. If your Super Bowl performance dictates your identity, a script develops and programs your psyche. The script says, "I am a failure. I am ashamed, and I should be." This structure spins your imagination toward worst-case scenarios in other areas of your life. Because you believe yourself to *be* a failure, you expect to fail in the future, not only in the football arena but everywhere you go.

Where might that lead? As long as the script is allowed to fuel negative expectations, it will dictate your story. You will unconsciously facilitate and live out the script. Without understanding why you are doing so, you will downsize your dreams. Worse, you will conclude that you were never all that you were cracked up to be. And because shame is involved, you will work to keep others from seeing how "wrong" you are as a human being.

The repercussions of such a viewpoint are many. Transparency in relationships becomes an overwhelming threat. Blame-shifting becomes an appropriate defense. Risk-taking is seen not as an inherent part of opportunity but as a guarantee of more shame.

Do you remember the connection between Mickey Mantle's home run statistics and his freedom to fail? Mantle knew that failure and success were bedfellows. For him to excel at the plate, he had to be willing to strike out. He gave himself permission to swing and miss, which he did more often than most players. Yet he was one of the most feared hitters in the game!

Consider your response to past failures. Have you worked so hard to eliminate the possibility of failing that you have also extinguished all chances of success?

There's alchemy for that.

What has been your view of failure up till now? Was your view accurate? Explain.

Leverage Your Failures

We can learn a lot from Mickey Mantle. He leveraged his failures in favor of his future. In other words, he used his strikeouts to increase his home run percentages and to create favorable future outcomes. His approach led to his ultimate induction into the Major League Baseball Hall of Fame. Mantle was as flawed as the rest of us, but when it came to hitting the ball, he knew the difference between failing and being a failure.

That is where the alchemy of change starts: with drawing a stark line between your performance and your essence. The two are not interchangeable. Regardless of what you have been taught or what you have accepted as fact, this truth is ironclad: *Your essence may change your performance, but your performance can never change your essence.*

Make a Mickey Mantle decision and give yourself permission to fail. Until you do, you are not really free to succeed. Accept failure for what it is: an integral part of achievement. When something you do goes haywire, face it. Instead of beating yourself over the head or sweeping your failure under the rug, ask yourself two questions: *What went wrong?* and *How can I do it better next time?*

Thomas Edison was an expert at this.

In developing a commercially viable light bulb, Edison actually went through over ten thousand prototypes before getting it right....Later Edison became famous for saying "I have not failed 10,000 times. I have not failed once. I have succeeded in proving that those 10,000 ways will not work. When I have eliminated the ways that will not work, I will find the way that will work."[8]

Edison did not even see his failures as failures! To him, they were a means of eliminating false solutions and isolating the right ones. He honored both his efforts and his person, and he kept on trying. Instead of souring on the mission, he simply accomplished it another way.

Edison's "failures" transformed the world, all because he saw failure as feedback. How much more enjoyable and prosperous might your life be if you did the same? When your efforts fail, you can be thankful to know what doesn't work. Then, you can be creative in finding the next—and possibly the perfect—iteration of your idea. That is where innovation comes from—working through ideas until the right combination leads you to a brand-new answer.

Such was the genius of Steve Jobs. He saw an opportunity to innovate the wireless industry and the cell phone. The integration of phone, computer, and iPod into a single user-friendly handset called the iPhone was a coup. It transformed industry standards and consumer expectations.[9] Every time a new iPhone is released, consumers stand in line for days and willingly lay down hundreds of dollars—*for a phone!*

Jobs' road to the iPhone was not easy. Apple "alchemists" worked under enormous pressure to introduce a new concept to the marketplace. The company's reputation and market share were at risk. Their efforts failed more than once. But they leveraged those failures, ultimately accomplished their mission, and transformed the industry.

Leveraging your failures can change your world.

The Alchemy of Creativity

The point was made in an earlier chapter that you are creative, whether or not you believe you are. You may not be a renowned artist, but that doesn't change the fact that you were born creative.

Not all creativity involves being artistic. Artists are important, but the world needs more than art to make it work. The point is that when you own your inherent creativity, you contribute to your world. You might even transform it! So, if you feel stuck in neutral or even in reverse, it's time to ask whether you know what creativity really is.

I have found that most people misunderstand creativity and confuse it with artistic output. For example, let's assume that you collect woven baskets. When you see one that is particularly beautiful, you might say, "This one is so distinctive. What creative work!" Although I would understand the intent behind your comment, I would have to call it inaccurate.

Artisans have been weaving baskets for thousands of years. Each basket is somewhat unique, but they are all baskets made according to common practices.

Do you see what I'm getting at? The work of a basket-weaver is not creative but duplicative. At its most fundamental level, a basket repeats a general process and design. To be creative is to *create* something that has no precedent, or at least is unprecedented at some level. That is what Apple did with the iPhone. They combined known ideas in a way that produced unknown potentialities. The marketplace, along with the nature of communication, shifted. Instead of wireless service giving value to the phone, the phone drove consumers to value certain networks—and Apple took a monthly cut of each consumer contract.[10] This was not the only innovation involved in the iPhone story; but even if it had been, it altered the communications landscape.

Many would say, "Yes, but that's Steve Jobs. He was a genius."

Somehow, we adopted the mistaken belief that creative genius is an aberration that shows up only once in a while in rare people like Steve Jobs. I submit to you that this is a lie. What separates most of us from Steve Jobs is a structure. It is the belief that copying someone's existing blueprint is safer than navigating the gap of innovation. Instead of exploring the blue sky for ourselves, we try to tap into a corner of another person's.

Steve Jobs refused to be a follower. He believed in his ability to create, and he used it. In February 2005, he told the wireless carrier Cingular that "Apple had the technology to build something truly revolutionary, 'light-years ahead of anything else.'"[11]

Jobs delivered on the promise. It was alchemy of the first order!

How does his story impact yours? The alchemy of change works the same way for you as it did for him. First, you must allow your ideas of creativity to be jostled. Then you must vet your lifelong assumptions. Pull up the weeds and adjust your thinking until it reflects the truth. And then, own the reality of *your* creativity—even if you see no sign that it exists.

It exists, all right. Adjust your vision, and you will see it.

The iPhone success story was birthed from a labyrinth of challenges, including price wars and market saturation. "Wireless access was no longer a luxury; it had become a necessity. The greatest challenge facing the carriers wasn't finding brand-new customers but stealing them from one another."[12] Steve Jobs and Apple found creative solutions wrapped inside the very problems plaguing the industry. The iPhone's popularity made it iconic and revolutionized the business model, forcing a wealth transfer from the carrier's income stream to Apple's coffers!

Mining Metaphors and Solutions

We have already discussed how you use metaphors to interpret what you see. You know, too, that your interpretations are filtered through your way of being, so that you see things as *you* are rather than as *they* are.

You are not alone in this. Our use of metaphors springs from our unique perceptions of self, circumstances, goals, and dreams. The more conscious we become about the metaphors we use, the better we understand how our lives work. The operative word here is *conscious*. The metaphors we choose are so embedded in our unconscious thoughts that we barely notice using or being affected by them.

The alchemy of change requires that we become more aware of our metaphors. This is how we begin to harvest information from them. Metaphors reveal our sense of the world and tell us why we interpret it as we do. They also show us how we organize our thoughts and why we do it so uniquely.

Fishing your metaphors from the soup of your unconscious is not that hard. Pay close attention to your speech, and the metaphors will pop out. They may sound something like the following:

My job is a war zone.

I feel like David in a world of Goliaths.

My life is always moving one step forward and two steps back.

Once you pinpoint a personal metaphor, ask yourself some questions. The following list will get you started:

+ What does this metaphor reveal about how I see things? (What beliefs, values, and emotions does it express?)

+ How does it reveal who I am or who I think I am? (How am I depicted?)

+ How does it express what I most want or most fear? (Does it reflect perceived opportunities or dangers, or both, and in what proportion?)

+ What does it say must happen for me to "get there from here"? (What challenges does it outline?)

+ What problems or barriers, real or perceived, does it reveal? (What enemies and/or hindrances does it name?)

+ What solutions does it suggest? (How can I creatively apply what the metaphor reveals?)

+ What does it reveal about my inner landscape? (Am I depicted as being confident? Fearful? Effusive? Retiring?)

These investigative questions will help you map the contours of your gap. Just stay curious and objective. Don't let hearsay or past experience tell you what works and what doesn't. Rather, let the metaphors point you to new and surprising solutions.

Remember, the alchemy of change is not the exclusive providence of those known as titans in their fields. They are sojourners, just like you. And, like them, you were created to transform the shadows into something brilliant.

Sounding the Depths

1. Describe the "lead" you see in your life and the "gold" it can be changed into. What would be the effect, to you and to others?

2. What does it mean to look beneath the sailboat? Give a specific example in your life.

3. How do the stories of the boy with the big ears and the man who believed he was ugly speak to you? How do they confirm or change your outlook?

4. Imagine that a particular "gatekeeper between your ears" is a person. What would you say to him or her? Do your words indicate a change in your perspective, or do they prompt change? Do they do both?

5. What has been your most painful failure? How, specifically, can you leverage it in favor of your future?

Notes

1. "The Magic and Myth of Alchemy," lloydlibrary.org, http://www.lloydlibrary.org/exhibits/alchemy/history.html.

2. "History of Alchemy," lloydlibrary.org, http://www.lloydlibrary.org/exhibits/alchemy/history.html.

3. Merriam-Webster Online, *Merriam-Webster Online Dictionary 2014*, s.v. "alchemy," http://www.merriam-webster.com/dictionary/alchemy.

4. Merriam-Webster Online, *Merriam-Webster Online Dictionary 2014*, s.v. "transmute," http://www.merriam-webster.com/dictionary/transmute.

5. Maxwell Maltz, M.D., F.I.C.S, *Psycho-Cybernetics* (New York: Prentice-Hall, 1960), 7.

6. Ibid.

7. Ibid., 30–31.

8. Nathan Furr, "How Failure Taught Edison to Repeatedly Innovate," *Forbes*, June 9, 2011, http://www.forbes.com/sites/nathanfurr/2011/06/09/how-failure-taught-edison-to-repeatedly-innovate/.

9. Fred Vogelstein, "The Untold Story: How the iPhone Blew Up the Wireless Industry," *Wired Magazine*, January 9, 2008, http://www.wired.com/gadgets/wireless/magazine/16-02/ff_iphone?currentPage=all.

10. Ibid.

11. Ibid.

12. Ibid.

9

Transition Mastery

Liminal spaces can be intimidating, but only until you become convinced of your innate capacity for gap navigation. Consider the following: How many times have you dreamed of that certain "someday" when your life will look the way you have always wanted it to look? How many times have you prayed, begged, and cried for certain changes to happen, only to experience extreme disappointment when they don't?

More than once, right?

Your desire for healthy change has persisted because you were built for it. You are a vessel designed to master transition in meaningful and powerful ways. You get antsy in stagnant waters, and you keep searching for greater challenges, because advancement is encoded in your DNA.

Nevertheless, you have probably encountered your share of the doldrums. But the call of destiny and purpose can be stifled for only so long. Even when you are lulled into the doldrums, you eventually long for the trade winds, for new shores.

Dorothy, the Gap Navigator

Classic fiction stories speak to our journeys in powerful and unthreatening ways. This is the reason we treasure them. In *The Wizard of Oz*, for example, Dorothy heard the call of life "over the rainbow." She had tired of her life in Kansas, so she imagined a more colorful place. Her metaphor revealed her belief in a perfect realm somewhere beyond her reach.

The story is full of symbolism. Do you remember when Dorothy's dog, Toto, escaped from Miss Gulch, the mean woman who had arranged for him to be euthanized? Her name literally means "a small, narrow valley with steep sides"[1]—in other words, *a rut*. Dorothy recognized her rut. Her use of a rainbow metaphor proves it. Yet she was restrained by human reasoning and other people's expectations. Toto was not. He did what Dorothy longed to do—he fled.

The little dog symbolized the instinctual side of human nature that resists the rules of the conscious mind and sees what the conscious mind misses. He escaped the rut, triggering a liminal experience that landed him and Dorothy in Oz.

Toto was not looking for a gap to navigate. He ran from Miss Gulch because he sensed trouble ahead. Dorothy knew how serious the trouble was, so she set out to rescue him. Yet it was Toto who drew Dorothy to the edge of her known world. In their shared liminal space, they met three other sojourners: the Scarecrow, the Tin Man, and the Cowardly Lion. All of them were searching. The Scarecrow needed a brain. The Tin Man needed a heart. The Cowardly Lion needed courage.

The Dorothy in You

Are our narratives so different from Dorothy's? Once we realize that we have narratives of our own, we discover that the answer is no. We each have our own Toto—a person or a situation that draws us to the threshold between the conscious and unconscious realms. And we are all like Dorothy in that we long for fulfillment and fiercely protect the people and possessions we love.

One fact we tend to overlook is that we are the Scarecrow, the Tin Man, and the Cowardly Lion, too. We want to make meaning of our world.

We get caught in storms that leave us rusted and paralyzed and needing someone to free our frozen joints. And we fight against self-limiting fears that keep us from confidently advancing toward our futures.

Even as we subconsciously resist change, we are all on the hunt for transition!

So, we press toward our version of Oz in search of the answers we need. The journey is exciting, but it is unnerving, too. It is unlike anywhere we have ever been or anything we have seen. Everything looks strange, and nothing works the way it used to. The place is all about thresholds that must be crossed and gatekeepers who must be faced down. It is a place of learning that old ways don't work in new lands. We don't know—we *cannot yet know*—how to function there.

But we must go.

Our "yellow brick road" takes us to an inward world. Like Dorothy, we're not in Kansas anymore. We are excited to leave the farm and explore new places, but we are shaken to learn that Auntie Em cannot protect us any longer. The lack of protection is unsettling but necessary. Until we are forced to function in spite of it, we cannot tap into our own capacities. Instead, we retreat without knowing that we could stand up to the Wicked Witch of the West and win.

The uneasy environment of the liminal space is a great teacher. Its pressures tutor us in fuller expressions of meaning and purpose. Yet we don't have to learn our lessons all alone. We take comfort in having the Scarecrow, the Tin Man, and the Cowardly Lion as our companions. Even so, we must understand that there are limits to what they can do for us. After all, they are at least as shaken as we are. One can barely stand, one is searching for what he believes, and the other is afraid of his own roar! Even the Wizard, who supposedly has all the answers, will test us and withhold his secrets until we are ready for advancement.

So, what has Oz got to do with your mastery of transition?

Everything. You are in a season and a space that is unwilling to cooperate with how you think your world should work. You have read this far in hopes that your current state would be confirmed. You still want to be convinced that you are not there alone. You have begun connecting the dots, but a few more connections are needed to bridge the gap between your former state and your future one. Even if the former state no longer fits in your world, it is familiar and comforting to think about it. Regardless of how amazing your future state will be, it feels foreign and somewhat forbidding at the moment. Thus, doubt lingers in your mind. You might already be convinced about where you are going, but you feel unsure that you can get there from here.

Why? Because the picture of your future tests you just as surely as the Wizard tested Dorothy. Its mere existence is provocative. It is bigger than you and demands a greater capacity than you have had to demonstrate in the past. If this weren't so, it would not be a picture of destiny; it would but a recycled blueprint for stagnation.

In the unstable atmosphere of your Oz, the test takes many shapes. The gatekeeper between your ears is your expert in-house examiner. Savvy as he is, he threatens you with a simple yet devastating negation: "You can't come in here."

You have heard that line before. You may even have taken it to heart. The coach in your pocket is here to set the record straight. He has a word, too: "Enough!"

You *can* come in here. You were born for this. Now you are going to show the Wizard how transition mastery is done.

> The bigger your dream, the weightier the responsibility required to carry it out. Learn to reflect on your strengths and weaknesses in healthy ways. Seek the wisdom of people who have traveled the path to authentic success. Interacting with them will enlarge your perspective. Your willingness to remain coachable will keep you attuned to significant moments and your own blue-sky opportunities.

The Oz Response

The urge to travel "over the rainbow" is a sign that you are hungry for transition. The status quo is not working and will never accommodate your dreams. What you need to do is to unbury old structures and rearrange them. Dreams, desires, gifts, and callings shrouded in layers of disappointment and disillusionment must be dusted off and put to work. Their season of dormancy—and yours—is over. Transition is straight ahead!

When your desired reality develops a clear voice, change will appear as the obvious solution. But even if you welcome it, change will provoke inner resistance. Remember, there is inherent tension between what your mind is doing and what it is fighting against. This "sustained incoherence"[2] incites resistance and makes change unappealing. Your most treasured beliefs and values prompt the same response. The more invested in them you are, the less you want to rethink them.

Before you ever see Oz, these blips will alert you to a transition in the making. Waves will kick up around you, and flotsam will litter your waters. But don't be alarmed. You already know that choppy waters and transition go together. Churning is necessary to bring the depths of your heart to the surface. In fact, this is what liminal spaces do best. They focus your attention on the hidden things that once controlled you. Remember, whatever you bury stays alive. Times of transition force buried things into your conscious space so you can control them and eradicate any negative effects they may have produced on your life.

By now, these coaching points are almost second nature to you, and you are ready to take on Oz. How do you respond to the place? A few good questions will help develop the right answers and position you to master the transition.

You will have questions of your own, so go ahead and add them to your list. The following three questions will prime the pump:

- What life outcomes do I want to realize? (What is my life *really* about?)

- What interim (transition) results do I want to achieve? (What steps signify real progress?)

- What do I want to create in this season of my life? (What am I building? What will it do? Who will benefit from it?)

You cannot stroll into Oz half-cocked. The Wizard is terse and dismissive. He won't respond to your requests until you prove you are in earnest and determined to follow your path. When you become committed to cooperating with your purpose, he, and all your "wizards," will climb on board.

> Your desire to close the gap between where you are and where you want to be will surely collide with the human tendency to preserve old patterns, even when they have outlived their usefulness. The greater the internal resistance you experience, the greater the inner work that needs to be done. Do not quit. The rewards will be great!

Mastery Basics

The threshold is the edge of the liminal space; transition is its halfway point. Dorothy and Toto reached the halfway point when they left Kansas and landed in the Technicolor place called Oz. The place posed the gap navigator's usual dilemma. Dorothy was bored with farm life, but she felt comfortable in it. Oz was more exciting, but it offered no comfort at all. The place was intimidating, unpredictable, and unwilling to accommodate her habitual ways of seeing and being.

That is the nature of transition. Its unbending rules and unreasonable demands require something you cannot give and could not manage, anyway. It is a place far enough above your previous pay grade to produce cold feet and a longing for the dull predictability of home. There is no formal boot camp in which to ramp up, and no way to tone the place down.

This is where you realize that you cannot reach your destination without help. Finding a mentor—someone to help you bridge the gap with understanding and expertise—is key. But you will need to be teachable. Like a pilot trusting his instruments in a blinding storm, you must trust the objective voices of experienced navigators. That will take humility. So, go ahead and surrender. Admit that you need help. Then accept the help you need.

A certain Bible story captures the essence of transition.[3] Jesus' disciples were sailing the Sea of Galilee to Capernaum. They began the journey at night, without their mentor, Jesus. Once the shore was lost in the darkness, a fierce wind roiled the sea. The storm was so violent that it stretched these

very experienced fishermen to the limits of their capabilities. After row-
ing three or four miles, they were far enough away from either shore to be
locked into transition. The only way out was *through*.

In every journey, there are destinations, goals, opportunities, and
transformations that want to happen, and other forces that resist them.
High winds opposed the disciples' objective to reach Capernaum in one
piece. The opposition also produced stress. One gospel account says the
men strained at the oars, against the wind.[4]

They continued to do the only thing they knew to do: *row*. Suddenly, no
doubt when they had reached their breaking point, their mentor appeared.
As if they hadn't already had the scare of their lives, Jesus came walking on
the water—the very water that threatened to cut off their future. Already
wracked by turmoil, they responded in fear, figuring that He was a ghost.

Mentors understand the stresses and strains of transition. Jesus
knew the disciples were in over their heads, so He comforted them. And
the instant He climbed into the boat, the wind ceased, and they were at
Capernaum![5]

Based on this gospel account, two points stand out: First, you should
expect turbulence in your transition. If you have ever moved from one
house to another, you know what transition looks like. It is a disorienting,
chaotic mess. Your usual organization becomes strained, and life flies off
the rails. Transition is, by nature, unsettled.

Second, notice that Jesus showed up at a pivotal moment. As the expression goes, When the student is ready, the teacher appears. When you
are ready to be helped and are teachable, help becomes available. The right
mentor can provide insight that shortens the span of your transition and
keeps you from wandering in circles. So, be willing to ask for the help
you need. But realize that your help comes in the right timing, which is
not necessarily your timing. If it came too soon, your habits of perception
would have screened it out, and precious insight would have been wasted.

Receiving insight and understanding is the liminar's choice. If you deny
reality or eject yourself from the liminal space, you will unconsciously bar
from your conscious thoughts the information you claim to desire. If you

embrace the experience, understanding will do its work. And when you reach your destination, you will refuse to take the credit.

In another experience at sea, Jesus quieted the storm, saying, *"Peace, be still"* (Mark 4:39). The ancient prophets before His time had a vision of peace as expressed in the Hebrew word *shalowm*, or *shalom*. It describes such wholeness that nothing is missing or broken. As you master transitions, the broken places in your life are restored, and greater depths of wholeness become yours.

The Realm of Anti-Structure

Do you remember Richard Rohr's quote about great achievers and their lives of chronic liminality? He said,

> Nothing good or creative emerges from business as usual....Most spiritual giants try to live lives of 'chronic liminality' in some sense. They know it is the only position that insures ongoing wisdom, broader perspective and ever-deeper compassion.[6]

The liminal space is a place of anti-structure. In order to benefit from it, you must embrace being undone. Previously built structures are subject to dismantling, and the rules that brought you to the threshold expire. Familiar processes that helped you navigate your life before the threshold can prove ruinous if you repeat them on the other side.

To master transitions, you must be willing to adapt. Even your way of being will be sifted. Habits of perception that have been proven untrustworthy in the liminal space must be released so that you may start redesigning. For example, if you are called to a place of leadership but are habitually passive and unused to taking the lead, the liminal space will force the contradiction to the surface. You will be made to deal with it or to accept a life of stagnancy.

If blame and victimhood are tempting substitutes for objectivity and responsibility, or if self-pity keeps you soaking in sorrow, let your transition strip them away. There is no room for excuses or artifices in your place of destiny fulfillment. When you are wronged, forgive and move on. If you are prone to manipulating circumstances and people to protect yourself against rejection and betrayal, drop the manipulation and risk the transparency that will allow you to bloom.

If old structures no longer fit, *tear them down*. Creative destruction is as much a part of transition as building is. Faulty beliefs and values will be exposed. Even your politics might come into question. What will you do if that happens? Will you stand on ceremony or reconsider?

If you truly desire to master your transitions, you cannot cling to what no longer fits. It does not matter how Mama, Uncle Frankie, and Great-Granddad voted. If you discover in the liminal space that your inherited ideas oppose the truth, you must decide which ideas you will honor. Everything you thought was set in stone will have to pass muster in transition. If you avoid the process, the only thing set in stone will be you.

The Place of Questions

Questions are vital to transition mastery. Do you know someone who would rather get lost than ask for directions? You're probably familiar with how that usually works out. In the liminal space, thinking you have it all figured out is futile. Meaning is essential. It must be sought, questioned, and settled. Until it is, discouragement threatens. The threat is not benign, either. Discouragement can convince you to abort your liminal crossing. It can coax you into an existential vacuum.

The uncertainty and flux of transition should force questions to bubble up in your conscious mind. They are part of the redesigning process the gap induces. Do you remember what happens in the midst of a rite of passage? The person participating in the ritual feels caught betwixt and between. The former state or status is over, but the new one is not yet fully accessible. Questions arise because being "in between" is uncomfortable. The discomfort is not unhealthy, however; it is an impetus to complete the ritual.

All transition produces the feeling of being "neither here nor there." *That is the liminal design.* The gap-crosser doesn't arrive at the threshold knowing the answers. He or she is in an alien space in which questions are the norm, and answers are not found until questions are embraced.

> Have you ever disqualified yourself from a new venture or experience because you did not know the answers? Do you see now that not knowing the answers is *not* a problem? Treat it as an opportunity to grow and expand your territory. When you do, new vistas will open before your eyes!

To ignore the questions that present themselves during times of transition is to forfeit the settling of issues that transition brings. Unless questions are raised and answered, wandering can become a way of life. Don't let "betwixt and between" become your permanent address!

Beware of Vision Drift

Even true liminars with strong vision experience fluctuations in the clarity of their vision. A far more serious issue is what I call "vision drift." (If left unchecked, vision drift becomes vision drag.) It sets in when you feel as if you are headed nowhere in particular. Often, this sense of listlessness happens when you reject an aspect of your journey or the rebuilding that it demands.

There is a coaching axiom for that: *You cannot allow what you won't accept.* The idea seems self-evident, but the conscious mind needs to process it. Any refusal to accept what shows up—whether good, bad, or ugly—is a refusal to process what must be processed. As long as such repression is enforced, vision remains on hold. Until you allow your internal and external states to be aligned and realigned as needed, your vision will be empty.

There is another danger to consider. Our natural tendency is to revert to chaos. Unless we accept and allow what must be seen and what wants to happen, we will experience disintegration and fragmentation instead of the wholeness we crave. Wholeness is both the goal and the gold in the alchemy of change. It is a state of integrity and internal congruence that is maintained day by day. It means having an attitude of lifelong learning, which, in turn, demands openness to internal and external adjustments.

Ask the Questions

Many questions arise during times of transition, but four specific queries are essential to its mastery and to wholeness:

+ Who am I? (This is not just a matter of identification but of identity, which includes destiny.)

+ Where have I come from? (This is more than a "where" question. It is about what your journey has signified to this point, and what deeper meaning it holds for your future.)

+ Why am I? (This question includes your purpose but also goes beyond it, to your inherent value as a human being. If you view the circumstances of your birth as being in any way "invalid" or "illegitimate," you are at cross-purposes with yourself. Such a structure must fall in order for your transition to be complete.)

+ Where am I going? (This question, too, is about more than location. It is about the life that has been prepared for you and about how your showing up affects others.)

Just as rites of passage square away old states and statuses and make the new ones official, these questions will help the seemingly chaotic transition to produce the healthy convergence that is waiting on the other side of the gap.

Don't Circle the Wagons

True liminars understand and respond to the real dangers they face. A powerful example is seen in early American exploration and expansion. Regardless of the historical and social questions that expansion raised, the early settlers took enormous risks to go west. Wagon trains braved all kinds of weather, terrain, and warfare. The only constant on the journey was the unknown. The trip was a cavalcade of liminal spaces.

The settlers were pilgrims who lived on the edge, both physically and metaphorically. Danger was everywhere, and survival was never guaranteed. Because the risks increased at night, pioneers would band together by arranging their wagons in a circle. Inside the circle, they would build campfires where the women cooked the meals and families socialized.

On the outer perimeter, men took turns guarding the camp against wild animals, marauders, and tribal warriors. Circling the wagons did not ward off all danger, but it offered the best protection possible.

The Conestoga wagons may be long gone, yet wagons are circled today, even if only metaphorically. What a powerful metaphor it is! "Circling the wagons" connotes the measures taken by organizations or factions when they come under attack. Whatever the onslaught, they band together from within to fend off the danger from without.

The term "circling the wagons" is usually used in a negative sense today, suggesting that the imperiled group is being scrutinized for its questionable actions or practices. The circling of wagons, then, implies the protection of secrets through propaganda and other scripted forms of communication.

Circling the wagons does not always indicate foul play, but always it invokes a reactionary, self-protecting posture. We "circle our wagons" when we are spooked by rising levels of uncertainty and insecurity. Millions circled their wagons after the economic crash of 2008. Small investors cashed out or reallocated their 401k assets, and many locked in their losses in the process. Consumers tightened their belts and postponed purchases large and small. Retailers streamlined their inventories. Companies enacted hiring freezes, and many slashed their payrolls.

Some reactions were sensible and wise. Others were purely driven by fear, causing more harm than good. All of them were efforts to circle the wagons and recreate a former sense of security that had since expired. In that kind of climate, few people had a blue-sky attitude toward life. Countless dreams were pushed to back burner, and many lives and businesses entered holding patterns that would last for years. While a measure of safety was achieved in some cases, forward thinking was largely stifled.

The economic dangers were very real. In 2008 alone, the United States lost $2.8 trillion of wealth in home equity and the stock market.[7] There was every reason to be cautious. Yet not everyone hit the pause button. Some viewed the uncertainty and contraction as an opportunity. These adventurers expanded their portfolios, often at discounted prices. They saw a liminal space crammed with risks and unknowns, and they dove in headfirst.

This was not child's play. The markets were teetering. The reports were dismal:

> The widely watched Dow Jones Industrial Average hit its all-time high on October 9, 2007, closing at 14,164.43. Less than 18 months later, it had fallen more than 50% to 6,594.44 on March 5, 2009.[8]

When markets plummet, most people withdraw from risk altogether. But the blanket avoidance of risk creates problems of its own, including stagnation and vision drag, as well as the longer-term losses that follow.

Many who cashed out learned how expensive their withdrawal from the markets could be. Since the market lows of 2009, stocks have rebounded. How long the numbers will stick is unknown, but those who held steady recovered most, if not all, of their losses. And when the Dow closed well above 16,000 on December 31, 2013, those who had expanded their positions were singing the markets' praises.[9]

Pulling back from thresholds and clinging to the status quo leads to vision drag. The condition is marked by small thinking and knee-jerk reflexes. It is much easier to contract than to cure. The following symptoms of vision drag, if left untended, can become chronic:

+ Blindness at the spiritual level, including a loss of connectedness to your world, to others, and to your place in the world

+ One-sided thinking and/or a lock-step and bunker mentality, in which the truth is no longer held in creative tension

+ Information without transformation (being aware of what is happening but making no inward progress and pursuing no innovative solutions

+ "Going through the motions" syndrome (talking the talk but lacking a real experience)

+ Dependence on rote routine and ritual (taking only safe, habitual steps that lack creative expression of self and of destiny)

Risk is not a goal unto itself. Protection and security certainly have their place. The strategy to risk *nothing* might sound comforting in seasons of loss. But it leads to other temptations. It perpetuates a resistance to moving forward and to believing that you can!

A Classic Case of Vision Drag

In his novel *Great Expectations*, Charles Dickens gives us the unforgettable character of Miss Havisham. She is a stark example of how *not* to master your transitions. Her reaction to emotional trauma locks her into the past and prompts her to lock others out of their futures.

> She is manic and often seems insane, flitting around her house in a faded wedding dress, keeping a decaying feast on her table, and surrounding herself with clocks stopped at twenty minutes to nine. As a young woman, Miss Havisham was jilted by her fiancé minutes before her wedding, and now she has a vendetta against all men. She deliberately raises Estella to be the tool of her revenge, training her beautiful ward to break men's hearts.[10]

Miss Havisham's loss was so painful, and her heart so broken, that she brought her world to a complete halt. Her strategy extinguished any hope of wholeness. She circled her wagons so completely that...

+ She became disconnected from the world, from healthy relationships, and from serving a fruitful role in society.

+ She turned her manor into a bunker from which she launched vengeful schemes.

+ She cut herself off from transformation and would not allow herself or anyone else to embrace love again.

+ She went through the motions, still breathing but not really living.

+ She enforced rituals that ensured stagnancy, and lost all expression of self and of her true destiny.

Miss Havisham refused to make the transition from being jilted to being unattached and free to marry someone else. She was less committed to living than she was to memorializing the unfairness of life.

Three Levels of Commitment

To become a master of transition, you must be willing to turn life's lemons into lemonade. When life goes contrary to your plan, your commitment to beneficial outcomes will help you to remain standing.

Not all commitment is created equal. Three general levels of commitment lead to three very different outcomes:

- Commitment Level 1: "I like it, and it will benefit me." (Miss Havisham liked the idea of marrying a certain man and believed it would produce the life she wanted. When the idea failed to produce the desired result, the lacked the commitment to make adjustments.

- Commitment Level 2: "I will support it as long as it's convenient." Miss Havisham supported the idea of marrying, as long as it was on her terms. When supporting the idea of marriage challenged her emotional rigidity, she made a more convenient choice: She sabotaged any hope of marriage for herself or her daughter, Estella.

- Commitment Level 3: "I will make any sacrifice necessary to make this happen." Miss Havisham was unwilling to sacrifice her self-pity, her victim status, and her desire for revenge; therefore, she thwarted any opportunities to find a bright future.

Being rejected by her fiancé thrust Miss Havisham toward a liminal space that was not of her own choosing. Had she been willing to navigate it, she might have married a good man and fulfilled her dreams. And whether she married or not, she would have become a better person in the long run. Instead, she worshipped her sense of rejection and poisoned others with it.

Anxiety in the Liminal Space

Part of Miss Havisham's struggle was no doubt related to something that shows up in every liminal space: *anxiety*. It strikes us at our very core and becomes the elephant in the room we wish to avoid. Yet anxiety is part and parcel of the liminal space.

Dealing with anxiety is anathema to us. So is admitting that we suffer from it. And so, we find creative ways to mask the pain. Miss Havisham's measures were extreme: She anesthetized herself by rejecting life and dismissing her expectations. She refused to move forward and focused on hurting others. Instead of dealing with her own anxiety, she made sure everyone else experienced some, as well.

Anxiety cannot be neatly tucked away. For one thing, it is a fact of life. For another, it serves a purpose in our liminal experiences. Anxiety flags the issues that are playing out under the surface, such as structures that contradict our purpose and beg for redesign. If we are willing to heed the signs and are committed to achieving positive outcomes, we will own the warnings and replace skewed structures with healthy ones.

To fulfill our destiny and *really live*, we have to stop wishing and start committing to a larger purpose that leaves us hungry to make whatever sacrifice is necessary for its fruition. Pride, convenience, and control must go. It is time to take our thresholds boldly, knowing that our real enemies are not "out there" but "in here."

Your Mastery Toolbox

If you are ready to master your current transition, as well as future transitions, the coach in your pocket has a specialized toolkit to share. Three simple tools will help you navigate and master every transition.

Strategy Tools to Help the Decision-Making Process

Whatever your dream is, whatever purpose you are called to, and whatever gaps you have navigated along the way—you have discovered information that was news to you. That "news" is critical to transition mastery.

Lifelong learning is an absolute must. Staying teachable and coachable will keep you moving forward with confidence. But you must learn to balance information with transformation. Don't let lifelong learning produce a lockbox of data in the attic of your mind. Apply what you learn. Be curious about where any new information fits with your purpose in life. Keep growing, and you will keep living.

Remain curious and adjust the way your life is organized to whatever relevant information you may find. For your life to be vibrant, it must be in a constant state of building and rebuilding. When a mentor offers insight, use it to unlearn old, ineffective habits. Unlearning will starve the "gatekeeper between your ears" and uncover any acts of self-sabotage. It will help you break detrimental patterns, freeing you to create new, life-giving ones.

Being efficient is good, but being effective is better. If you are an efficient songwriter, you will write large numbers of songs. But if you are an effective songwriter, you will write unforgettable songs that affect large numbers of people!

> Miss Havisham chose to be "satisfied" with old news. Therefore, she lived quite literally in the past, even cultivating and preserving evidence of decay to support her data. She rendered herself incapable of making decisions to shape a positive future. Even changing her clothing was impossible. Although she still drew breath, she was not living.
>
> How might she have used her strategy tools to alter her situation?

Change-Management Tools to Help Locate Yourself

Always know where the red arrow is that says, "You are here." Remember that accurately defining your location is critical to reaching your destination. Starting where you really are is different from starting where you think you are. The former sheds light on your forward journey and creates a sense of confidence about the future. The latter keeps you wandering, backtracking, and squandering resources and energy.

Having a firm grip on where you are sharpens your vision, improves your credibility, bolsters your support system, and helps to define where you fit. Again, it is not a matter of *fitting in* but of *fitting with*. The distinction is subtle but meaningful. If you have ever assembled a jigsaw puzzle, you know that each puzzle piece serves two functions. One is *fitting in*, so that a certain piece fills a space of a particular size and shape. The second function is to *fit with* the rest of the puzzle, so that the color and pattern of the piece work with the surrounding pieces, not just to close a gap but to complete the picture, giving the puzzle meaning.

Those who use their change management tools can see the larger picture of both their current reality and their desired reality. They manage their development, not in constraining, obsessive-compulsive ways, but in ways that cause expansion and progress. They open up life's pathways by opening themselves to communication and feedback. They understand that they don't have all the answers, but, in fitting with others, they gain greater access to new locations, information, and resources.

Miss Havisham misread her location. When she was jilted, she judged herself to be at the end of meaningful life, controlled by disappointment, and hemmed in by unfulfilled expectations. In reality, she had suffered a significant setback—nothing more and nothing less. As painful as it was, her loss did not need to signal the death of her dreams. But once she decided that being abandoned was the end, she discounted change as a viable option. From that point forward, either fitting with anyone else or fitting in any other situation was contrary to her purpose, which was simply to memorialize her loss and to replicate it in others.

How might she have used her change management tools to restore wholeness and enable herself to enjoy her life?

Clarity Tools for Direction and Guidance

Every life story includes events that directly impact one's destiny: a door that opens to a new career, an unexpected relocation, the miraculous survival of a potentially fatal event, the birth of a child, the release of a first hit record. Some of these events occur according to the plans we have made, while others seem to happen spontaneously, even without our help. In either case, they are formative, catalyzing chains of events and helping us to understand who we are, where we are going, and why we have been called there.

Biographies describe destiny events, but always in the past tense. Our destiny events are lived in the present, and they are most transformative when we embrace them in the now. Viewing them while fully present in the moment allows us to not only enjoy our destiny events but also to learn from them. They provide us with information that is "hot off the press" to answer our past and present questions, as well as clarify our steps toward the future.

For example, if you are a parent, you can probably remember the first time you held your child in your arms. In that sublime moment, countless thoughts ran through your mind. You realized that this life was no longer all about you. You realized how precious and miraculous life is. Holding your baby may have put to rest old questions about whether and when you should become a parent, whether you could handle change, or whether your life would have value beyond your final breath.

The parenting example is almost universal, but every destiny event is unique. Your destiny events tell a story distinct from anyone else's. When you catch on to their uniqueness, you begin to see your life in a revelatory light that produces pivotal points of decision with precision timing. These are now-or-never moments; they have no shelf life, no guarantee that they will come again. When you have the clarity to recognize them, they have the power to change your life.

Being truly alive to your points of decision takes belief—belief in your story, belief your journey, belief in the things you were created to do. Your belief comes from many sources, including the dreams you hold dear, the insights of your mentors, the stories of others, and even the needs that arise in your environment. So, cultivate a hearing ear—an expectant ear—that is tuned to the sound of transformation.

> Miss Havisham was so focused on a single destiny event that when it went awry, she could not imagine having others. She lacked belief in her story and failed to register its length and breadth. Instead, she measured her entire lifetime by a single, negative outcome.
>
> How might Miss Havisham have used clarity tools to her advantage? How might they have spared her from her "living death"?

Transition mastery empowers you to manage the uncertainties you will face in the gap. Instead of worrying about the *what-ifs* and questioning your capabilities, you will trust the next step. When the seas rise, you won't toss your confidence overboard. Rather, you will tack upwind and let transition open up new realms of understanding. Instead of succumbing to intimidation, you will face your fears and gain what cannot be found in comfortable spaces—the resilience that only gap living can produce.

Navigator, you are up for this!

Sounding the Depths

1. Who or what is your "Toto"—the person or situation drawing you to the threshold between the conscious and unconscious realms? How does "Toto" help to define the transition you are about to master?

2. What forms of resistance are showing up in your transition quest? What do they indicate about the inner work that needs to be done?

3. Reflecting on the past, can you identify any examples of times when you have reverted to chaos? Describe those experiences and explain how your approach stifled integration and wholeness.

4. Probe your current reality for any signs that you have "circled the wagons." Does a pattern emerge? How might you "uncircle" these wagons?

5. Pinpoint any current areas of anxiety. What does your anxiety reveal about what is happening in your inner life? How can this transition information be used to produce transformation?

Notes

1. Merriam-Webster Online, *Merriam-Webster Online Dictionary 2014*, s.v. "gulch," http://www.merriam-webster.com/dictionary/gulch.
2. Bohm, *Thought as a System*, 11.
3. See Matthew 14, Mark 6, and John 9.
4. See Mark 6:48.
5. See John 6:21.
6. Richard Rohr, "Days without answers in a narrow space."
7. John Carney, "America Lost $10.2 Trillion in 2008," Business Insider, February 3, 2009, http://www.businessinsider.com/2009/2/america-lost-102-trillion-of-wealth-in-2008.
8. Kimberly Amadeo, "Stock Market Crash of 2008," About.com U.S. Economy, http://useconomy.about.com/od/Financial-Crisis/a/Stock-Market-Crash-2008.htm.
9. Ben Rooney, "Stocks: Stellar Year Ends on a High Note," CNN Money, December 31, 2013, http://money.cnn.com/2013/12/31/investing/stocks-markets/.
10. "Great Expectations," SparkNotes, http://www.sparknotes.com/lit/greatex/characters.html.

Metamorphosis

You've come a long way, navigator! No, you haven't arrived. Sojourners never do. There is always another gap for you to navigate, another facet of your purpose to discover. But you have learned how to tack upwind. You are alive on the threshold and less intimidated by its rough edges. You are becoming more of who you were created to be, and you are starting to understand why things don't work the way they used to. You are acclimating to gap living—even appreciating the discomfort that says, "New things are ahead."

Understanding from the Inside Out

Your gap experience is anything but happenstance. Your internal states are linked to external events. They work in tandem to advance your story. And, like life itself, they must be understood from the inside out.

Your arrival at the gap is linked to your internal state. You have spent your entire life making sense of signs and symbols and monitoring the currents within your soul. Before the gap was evident, you sensed the shifting of the tectonic plates of your existence. Your way of being was challenged. Your responses were uncertain. Change was coming, and you somehow knew that it was time. You would not have asked for the gap to appear, yet the deepest parts of you knew that everything else led you here.

Now you *must* make the crossing.

Your soul is experiencing simultaneous excitement and dread. Its fundamental structure—again, often defined as the mind, the will, and the emotions—contains conscious and unconscious elements with structures of their own that govern your potential and influence your way of being. Whether these structures are patterns or images, they are operating at a deep level to affect the way you respond, react, and behave.

You don't arrive at the gap because your potential is spent. The gap is about potential yet to be utilized. Your soul is waving red flags, saying, "I am yet not where I want to be. Current reality is falling short. Something must change!"

When growth is the goal, change is inevitable. So is resistance. Whether you are consciously aware of a shortfall or picking up unconscious signals of something amiss, structures of disappointment and denial will protest your advancement and pronounce your destiny—the full expression of your identity—*impossible*. And they will demand your agreement.

Navigator, do not listen to their lies. To agree with them is to allow your destiny to be denied. There is work to be done, but you are ready. Some structures need to be rearranged. Others need to be brought down. But you know how to do that now. You know how to clear your pathway. And the structures that have lain dormant—you must call them into service.

You are ready for metamorphosis.

Caterpillar No More

Metamorphosis is a pattern common in the physical and spiritual realms alike. Schoolchildren first grasp the concept when they learn about the process by which a caterpillar turns into a butterfly.

The definition of the word *metamorphosis* sounds too drab for the wonder it describes:

> ...a profound change in form from one stage to the next in the life history of an organism, as from the caterpillar to the pupa and from the pupa to the adult butterfly.[1]

One word from that definition hints at the miracle. That word is "profound." Metamorphosis is nature's brand of extreme alchemy. It changes what seems incapable of changing into something incapable of being ignored. When metamorphosis calls, change is irresistible. An observer describes its pull:

> From morning to late afternoon I watched a caterpillar climb a tall pine tree, climb without ever stopping to rest....This tiny creature spent the entire day climbing, up and up the tall rugged trunk, over hill and dale, then out along a high branch, never resting. He seemed to be feeling some urgency I thought; who knows? I've not been a caterpillar.[2]

The caterpillar was on a mission that was not of his own choosing. Yet the urgency of it was apparent. He dropped everything and followed the strange call.

> He was certainly determined. When he stopped, I thought he must be exhausted, and then he began to spin. Surely, he felt he was about to fall apart; how could he not? Did he know he was packing an incorruptible set of memories of lessons he had learned? And did he know about the imaginal discs that would transform him to something unrecognizable that would still be him living his life?[3]

More accustomed to slinking on his belly than twirling in midair, the caterpillar danced in circles and incarcerated himself in the dark cell produced by his spinning.

Mr. Caterpillar had officially departed the state of business as usual. Could he have known where his journey would lead? I cannot imagine so. But he knew that he must go where "there" was. So, he surrendered. He accepted isolation in the caterpillar version of the liminal space.

The outcome of the creature's willingness was unknown to him. Yet, without contract or guarantee, he went all in. That is part of the miracle! Of course, he was in good hands. His Maker knew what would happen. He knew the creeper would fly. But first, he had to navigate the gap between his old identity and a new one.

The results were beautiful, but the process was messy. The brave caterpillar squirted enzymes inside his cocoon. They digested his body and turned him into a spoonful of nutrient-rich primordial soup.

He looked nothing like a butterfly.

Imaginal Disks

Like a tiny "nowhere man," the caterpillar undergoing metamorphosis has no idea where he is going or what he will become. Yet within his dissolved remains are tiny structures of potential—his *imaginal disks* (also spelled *discs*). They know exactly what to do. They pre-imagined it!

> ### i·ma·gi·nal disk
> "A thickening of the epidermis of an insect larva, which, on pupation, develops into a particular organ of the adult insect."[4]

A caterpillar's imaginal disks are like embryonic cells. They are present inside the caterpillar throughout his life, yet they stop growing at a certain point and lie dormant until he is ready for transition. When the time comes, the disks "wake up" and direct the process. Since their inception, they have carried the butterfly code. They know exactly what parts are needed and where each one belongs. So, the information does its work to realize the liquefied creature's potential.

This is what imaginal disks are wired to do. Some of them become legs. Some form wings. Others become internal organs. And still others sprout antennae. The disks are so smart that if one wing disk is destroyed, the remaining three will compensate by becoming bigger wings.

New Brain, Old Memories

Although the caterpillar dissolved himself, an important part of his essence remained. Scientists now believe that butterflies and moths retain some of the memories developed in their earlier configuration. Brandon Keim writes:

> When a caterpillar turns into a butterfly, the transformation is so radical that it's hard to believe they belong to the same species. But

regardless of the new wings and body, the new diet and airborne lifestyle, butterflies remember what they learned as babies. In a study published…in *Public Library of Science ONE*, Georgetown University biologists gave mild shocks to tobacco hornworm caterpillars while exposing the caterpillars to particular odors. After the hornworms built cocoons and emerged as moths—a process that involves the reorganization of both brain and nervous system—they still avoided the smells that once brought them shocks.[5]

The creature is transformed, yet it remains itself at an essential level. It behaves differently, and the neighbors might not recognize it. But some of its memory-forming neurons are now part of its new, more complex brain. The butterfly is the proud new owner of a set of wings, but it probably remembers a thing or two about crawling.

Tomb as Womb

The almost complete demise of the caterpillar is accomplished through a host of concurrent transformations that play out in a peculiar caterpillar "tomb." The caterpillar enters it voluntarily and even builds it for itself. But inside its walls, the caterpillar disintegrates.

The caterpillar never exits the tomb. It loses all control of its condition and comes apart. It cannot defend itself or change its mind. Nothing works the way it used to, and the caterpillar cannot see what its options are. It is at the mercy of forces it does not understand. The observer I quoted earlier describes the process in terms that we can identify with, even though we have never hung in literal cocoons: "The transformations feel like death because they are deaths, and every life requires many deaths."[6]

Change is often painful. Yet, for the caterpillar, what looks very much like death is, in reality, a second birth. The caterpillar's cocoon is as much a womb as it is a tomb! Inside, the cells are hard at work. And even though the dissolved creature is unable to perform the functions once considered normal, its imaginal disks are doing things the creature never dreamed possible. Yes, the caterpillar form is lost forever, but a beautiful winged body will soon make its debut.

Our little sojourner did its part. It pushed its body uphill and submitted itself to the darkness of an unknown place. It entered an unfathomable transition and allowed its structures to be dismantled for the sake of its ultimate potential. By answering the call, the caterpillar turned its tomb into a womb.

Life in Your Cocoon

Can you relate to the caterpillar? Does your gap look messy? Do you feel as though your life is dissolving into pieces that can never be reconnected?

You did not ask for transformation, and certainly not for a tomb. You dreamed of changes that would come someday, but your blueprint looked much different. You were living your life in ways that seemed perfectly normal. Your "caterpillar" routines were familiar. You knew where to find food, and while you faced a fair number of challenges, they were the type to which you had grown accustomed.

Then came the gap, and all the rules changed. Your caterpillar habits stopped serving your purpose. The distance between your expectations and your current reality became wider than you thought. Your compartmentalization broke down day by day, until you found yourself hanging upside down, spinning. As though by special delivery, your tomb appeared, and your old life was laid to rest, leaving you with no hint of what was coming next.

This was not your idea of transformation. Now, the gooey mess seems like a terrible mistake. Your cocoon lighting stinks, and your control panel is missing. You cannot back out, and you cannot go forward until you agree to become a butterfly. What that means for the long term, you don't know. Will your new status be welcomed by your caterpillar friends? Or will you have to start all over again with a new crowd?

Suddenly, the lessons you learned in "caterpillar school" seem terribly out of place.

And yet, your disintegrated structures are nourishing your new life. Your tomb is truly a womb, rich with the nourishment you need to become the person you have longed to be. The threshold you unconsciously avoided is now being crossed, and your imaginal disks are creating a person who was always destined to fly.

Relationships, from the Womb Forward

To leave the caterpillar life behind, your habits of perception must take on a new shape. You must redefine your sense of mission and purpose based on a renewed sense of identity. You don't dissolve and resurrect with wings just to crawl on your belly again. The people and places you used to *fit with* now resist your new purpose. You underwent transformation, but they were not in the cocoon with you.

So, who are the butterflies with whom you need to fly? They are the ones who are supportive of your progress. Some may be mentors who can help you navigate new spaces. Others will be peers whose own sense of security and fulfillment allows them to embrace your new status.

Finding these other "butterflies" means sorting through the caterpillars—the people whose unconscious objections to your transformation make them unsupportive of it and of you. They fear change and are more comfortable with the "old you." Instead of being inspired by your new set of wings and your accompanying confidence, they feel threatened by them. You could win back their support, but only by crawling on your belly again. Your surrender would vicariously free them to continue denying the call of change in their own lives.

Having wings will test your mettle. Will you make the hard choices and refuse to accommodate a caterpillar mentality? Or will you allow toxic relationships to effectively clip your wings?

Oscillating or Advancing?

Sir Isaac Newton said that a body in motion tends to stay in motion. For the liminar, the specific kind of motion matters, and forward motion is essential. There is no transformation without it. Unless forward motion continues, even the benefits of transformation will degrade. Remember that our natural tendency is to revert to chaos. Therefore, we must allow our destiny events to emerge and unfold. If we resist them, disintegration and fragmentation are guaranteed.

Robert Fritz describes two contrasting patterns of movement: oscillation and advancement. Notice how one neutralizes progress while the other builds upon it:

> There are two basic structural patterns people have: advancing and oscillating. Advancing is a structure in which the success you have achieved becomes the platform for future success. You can build momentum over time, and the sum total of your life experiences leads you forward. In an oscillating structure the success you have created is neutralized. Each step forward is followed by a step backward. Within this structure, success cannot succeed long term. If you try to change your life and you are in an oscillating structure, success will only be temporary.[7]

Fritz explains the value of life experiences and their application to continued success. You don't leave the cocoon knowing all you will ever need to know. However, you must take what you do know and remain committed to advancement.

The butterfly cannot continue solely on the basis of its caterpillar memories. But it can take those memories and apply them in new ways. That is part of lifelong learning. When new opportunities appear, or old problems resurface, respond as a butterfly: Flap your wings and make internal shifts that are consistent with your new status. See your opportunities not as failures in the making but as new venues for fulfillment. See your problems not as issues to fix but as puzzles with pieces yet to be discovered. Change your posture from one of restlessness and dread to one of curiosity for adventure and creativity.

You did not exit the womb just to oscillate back and forth. Being in motion yet going nowhere is not your mission. You have wings that allow you to move in the direction of your dreams, regardless of any impediments on the ground. You crossed the threshold to reach someplace you have never been before. Don't be satisfied to maintain, but be content to work with the tools you have at hand. Day by day, new pieces will come together, and the picture of your future will become more and more complete.

A word to the wise: Even with your wings, the biggest potential block to living the ascended life is your perception of yourself and of your secret fears. If they are not healed, you are not whole. Don't recreate a caterpillar lifestyle by dragging unhealed perceptions up to the new heights you have reached. If you attempt this, you will project who you thought you were onto the butterfly you have become.

In other words, instead of advancing, you will oscillate back and forth. Robert Fritz explains that structure determines whether you oscillate or advance. He then describes oscillation and its remedy, which you already know how to apply:

> With oscillation, the tendency is to swing back and forth between competing goals such as change and stability or short- and long-term growth. If there is advancement, the tendency is to consistently move forward with each achievement serving as a foundation for further achievements. By examining the structures in play and utilizing the creative process, you can replace your oscillating structures with advancing ones.[8]

Metamorphosis as a Rite of Passage

Instinctively, we yearn for metamorphosis. Even without knowing why, the caterpillar places itself in a position to be transformed. Initiates in tribal rituals do the same thing. Like the caterpillar, they do not know precisely how to move from one state to another. Their job is mainly to show up.

Once the initiates present themselves, the elders do the work of imaginal disks: They carry information (the "trustful truth of the tribe") and guide the liminars from one status to the next. With an open heart, the initiates exchange their self-will and preconceived notions for their mentors' guidance and the requirements of the ritual. In submitting, they ensure their passage.

Like a rite of passage, metamorphosis draws a bright line between what came before and what is now. Until the process is complete, however, both statuses are inaccessible. This is the liminal space—the gap where initiates are caught betwixt and between. Like caterpillars digested in their own enzymes, they cannot be reconstituted into their former state. Nor can they function in their new one.

Completed rites of passage create certainty. When the ritual is complete, initiates have a clear sense of identity, along with documentation to prove that they have been transformed. Like newly minted butterflies, they know who they are and what they were created to do. They also know who they are *not*. They are not caterpillars anymore, and they do not crawl.

They *fly*.

Your Journey in Stages

To everything, there is a season—a stage to be embraced and then released so that the next stage can be lived. Four general stages mark your journey. You have seen them play out in your gap navigation so far, and you can also spot them in the larger scheme of your life.

As we summarize our journey through these pages, let's take a look at these four stages.

Crisis

Crisis is the game-changing event or condition that disrupts the status quo, causes disorientation, and prompts a reassessment of environment, perceptions, progress, patterns, way of being, and other structures.

A crisis is not necessarily a negative experience, although it could be a traumatic event, such as a divorce or an illness. It could also be a career change, a sudden societal shift, or the decision to marry. These major events force the sojourner to revisit and reconsider what he or she previously accepted as reality. From this analysis, new strategies, goals, and objectives are formed. Existing structures are rearranged or removed. New structures are set in place to support the updated sense of destiny and purpose.

Process

Process involves the sense of unease and anxiety that arises when crisis makes clear that change is imminent. Process is a valley of shadows where comfort and familiarity become scarce and uncertainty and alienation flourish, seemingly to your detriment.

Like the caterpillar that realizes it is being decomposed in the cocoon, the sojourner in process realizes that the past cannot be retrieved. What was once is no more, and what is ahead is not known. There is a sense of loss and even remorse, coupled with the fear that an already distressing experience could spiral downward into utter disaster.

Passage

Having realized that turning back is not an option, the sojourner considers another option: The only way *out* is *through*. There can be no ejection from the primordial soup. Leaving the process now would produce the worst of all possible outcomes. The ritual must be completed, the new status attained. It is the only remaining option. This sense of inevitability penetrates the resistance to change and brings the liminar into agreement with a larger purpose.

Portal

The portal is a liminal place where the end of the "nowhere zone" meets the threshold of a whole new world. This is where your new wings and expanded point of view go to work discovering new realms of opportunity and producing outcomes that are consistent with the destiny you have now embraced.

This is the place where dreams become reality and possibility overtakes doubt. The question becomes, *What is required of me in this new world?*

And that, dear butterfly, is a question for a future book.

Sounding the Depths

1. From personal experience, give an example of how internal states are linked to external events.

2. Are you ready to go "all in," even though metamorphosis is messy? What gives you pause? What upsides encourage you?

3. Do you have a personal experience you can relate to the caterpillar's experience in the cocoon? Can you identify ways in which your "tomb" was or is really a "womb"?

4. Identify those people in your life who are more comfortable with caterpillars than with butterflies. Explain. In whom might you invest more time and find more "butterfly affinity"?

5. In what ways are you oscillating, and in what ways are you advancing? Explain.

Notes

1. Dictionary.com Unabridged, Random House, Inc., s.v. metamorphosis, http://dictionary.reference.com/browse/metamorphosis.

2. Anne Benvenuti, "Imaginal Discs and Memories," The New Archaic (blog), September 27, 2013, http://newarchaic.net/?p=547.

3. Ibid.

4. Oxford Dictionaries, Oxford University Press, http://www.oxforddictionaries.com/us/definition/american_english/imaginal-disk.

5. Brandon Keim, "Butterflies Remember What They Learned as Caterpillars," *Wired*, March 5, 2008, http://www.wired.com/wiredscience/2008/03/butterflies-rem/.

6. Benvenuti, "Imaginal Discs and Memories."

7. Robert Fritz, "Structures," Robert Fritz Inc., http://www.robertfritz.com/index.php?content=principles.

8. Ibid.

About the Author

Mark J. Chironna has been in the people helping business for more than four decades. With a media presence spanning almost 175 nations, his message of wholeness through the integration of the spiritual and psychological is heard across the globe. He has a father's heart for emerging generations and serves as the presiding bishop of Legacy Edge Alliance, a worldwide fellowship of senior apostolic leaders and churches. Dr. Chironna is regarded as an influential leader whose global reach, clarion voice, and prophetic insight are respected by leaders and followers alike. He holds multiple advanced degrees in theology and psychology, and is the founder and senior pastor of Church on the Living Edge in Orlando, Florida. He and his wife Ruth have two adult sons and three grandchildren.

Notes

Notes

Notes

Notes

Notes

Notes

Notes

Notes

Notes

Notes

Welcome to Our House!

We Have a Special Gift for You

It is our privilege and pleasure to share in your love of Christian books. We are committed to bringing you authors and books that feed, challenge, and enrich your faith.

To show our appreciation, we invite you to sign up to receive a specially selected **Reader Appreciation Gift,** with our compliments. Just go to the Web address at the bottom of this page.

God bless you as you seek a deeper walk with Him!

WE HAVE A GIFT FOR YOU. VISIT:

whpub.me/nonfictionthx

WHITAKER
HOUSE